THE TACTICAL GENIUS:

ARNE SLOT'S JOURNEY TO LIVERPOOL

◇ REGINA BRAIDEN ◇

" Arne Slot: "Everybody tells me that a top Premier League table team is harder to beat than a bottom league table team... and we have NOT faced one of them yet".

> > >Liverpool won at Old Trafford against Man United".

DISCLAIMER

The views, opinions, and experiences shared in this memoir are those of the author, Regina Braiden, and do not necessarily reflect the views of any individuals, organizations, or institutions mentioned within the book. The events and personal insights contained in this memoir are based on the author's research, interviews, and interpretation of Arne Slot's career and coaching philosophy. While every effort has been made to ensure accuracy, the author cannot guarantee the complete accuracy or exhaustiveness of the information presented.

This book is a work of non-fiction and aims to provide inspiration and insight into the life of Arne Slot as a coach, leader, and figure in the world of football. All names, events, and experiences depicted are presented for educational and motivational purposes, and any resemblance to actual persons or events, living or dead, is purely coincidental unless otherwise stated.

TABLE OF CONTENTS

INTRODUCTION

It's difficult to pinpoint the exact moment when football stopped being just a game to me. Perhaps it was the first time I stepped onto the field with my youth team, feeling the weight of expectations mingled with the thrill of competition. Or maybe it was during my days at AZ Alkmaar, where I began to understand that coaching wasn't just about tactics, but about people—about the lives we shape through our commitment to something greater than ourselves. But what I do know is that my journey, both as a player and as a coach, has been a continuous evolution of learning, adapting, and striving to make a difference.

When I made the transition from playing to coaching, it wasn't an easy decision. The world of football management is not for the faint of heart. It's demanding, filled with highs and lows, and sometimes it feels like you're never quite in control. Yet, this uncertainty has always fueled my passion. I've come to realize that true leadership is about fostering relationships, inspiring resilience, and understanding that success doesn't happen overnight.

Looking back, my time at clubs like Feyenoord, AZ Alkmaar, and now Liverpool, has been a testament to the power of belief—belief in my players, belief in my methods, and belief in the potential of football to change lives. From the early days of my career to the pivotal moments that defined my coaching philosophy, this memoir is not just a recount of matches won or tactics deployed. It's a reflection on how I've shaped my identity as a coach, the lessons I've learned from the game, and the ways in which football, above all else, has taught me to keep pushing forward, no matter the challenges.

This is my story—not just the trophies, the wins, or the setbacks—but the journey that has led me to this point, and the journey that lies ahead. And I hope, in sharing it, I can offer something more than just a chronicle of my career. I want to offer the wisdom I've gained along the way, for players, coaches, and fans alike. Because football, in the end, is more than just a sport—it's a school for life.

Arne Slot on Chelsea : *I said before the game, and I said after the game, and I can say it one more time, a lot of people in England at the start of the season made a bit of fun about them investing so much money, and all these players that were not in the squad.*

But in my opinion, they've done in the last one or two years, really well bringing so many talented players in and now having such a strong squad with such a good manager, that they will be up there in the upcoming years. That's my opinion. And let's see if I'm right." □□

Is he right ?

CHAPTER 1

◇◇◇◇

Arne Slot, a figure of immense admiration in the footballing world, has roots deeply embedded in the soccer-rich culture of the Netherlands. Born on September 17, 1978, in Bergentheim, Slot's upbringing shaped his passion for football from a tender age. Bergentheim, located in the eastern province of Overijssel, was a town where the love of football coursed through everyday life, a characteristic feature of Dutch society. It was here that Slot's early fascination with the sport began to develop into a genuine calling.

Slot grew up in a supportive family, where his parents, Fennie and Arend Slot, nurtured his budding interest in football. As a young boy, Slot was not merely content with watching football; he immersed himself in the game, playing tirelessly with friends in local parks and school playgrounds. By the time he was old enough to join an organized youth team, it was clear that football was more than just a pastime for him; it was a way of life. He exhibited a natural understanding of the sport and quickly became known for his technical abilities and sharp tactical awareness. Coaches and peers alike marveled at his insight into the game, even in his formative years.

The Netherlands has long been celebrated for its contributions to football, both in terms of player development and tactical innovation. It is a country that produced legendary football figures like Johan Cruyff and Louis van Gaal, and Slot's early exposure to the principles of "Total Football" undoubtedly influenced his understanding of the sport. This strategic and fluid approach to football, which emphasizes adaptability and positional play, became a fundamental part of the Dutch coaching ethos. Growing up in this environment, Slot absorbed these principles, and they later informed his distinctive coaching philosophy.

Slot began his professional playing career at FC Zwolle, a club that would play a significant role in his development. FC Zwolle, now known as PEC Zwolle, was where Slot honed his skills as a midfielder. During his time there, he was known for his ability to read the game and make strategic plays, attributes that were instrumental in his successful career as a midfielder. His playing career spanned several clubs, including NAC Breda and Sparta Rotterdam, where he consistently demonstrated his tactical acumen and leadership qualities on the pitch.

Slot's years as a player were not without their challenges, but his perseverance and commitment to learning set him apart. He was a consistent and reliable presence in the midfield, known for his ability to dictate the tempo of the game and anticipate opponents' movements. These skills laid the groundwork for his transition into coaching, where understanding the nuances of player positioning and tactical formations would become crucial.

By the time Slot retired from playing, he had already developed a strong reputation for his football intelligence. His love for the game and desire to influence it from a different angle motivated him to take up coaching. Slot's first coaching experiences came at PEC Zwolle, where he began working with the academy, imparting his knowledge to young players. His work at the academy level was marked by a focus on developing not just technical skills but also the tactical awareness that had defined his own career.

In 2014, Slot became co-head coach at SC Cambuur, a role that significantly boosted his profile as a coach. At Cambuur, he showcased his ability to maximize team performance, implementing innovative strategies that emphasized possession-based football and tactical flexibility. His success at Cambuur earned him further recognition and set the stage for future opportunities at the top levels of Dutch football.

Slot's reputation grew when he joined AZ Alkmaar as an assistant coach in 2017, before being promoted to head coach in 2019. At AZ, Slot's coaching style truly came to the fore. He transformed the team into one of the most exciting sides in the Eredivisie, known for their attacking flair and disciplined defensive organization. His philosophy, heavily inspired by the Dutch tradition of fluid, total football, combined with his penchant for adaptability, led AZ to impressive finishes in the league. The club's performances under Slot attracted attention both domestically and across Europe, with many praising his tactical ingenuity and ability to develop young talent.

In 2021, Slot took on a new challenge as the head coach of Feyenoord, one of the most historic and successful clubs in Dutch football. His impact at Feyenoord was immediate, as he led the team to a series of strong performances in both domestic and European competitions. Slot's tenure at Feyenoord further cemented his status as one of the brightest coaching minds in the game. His emphasis on high-intensity pressing, quick transitions, and intricate attacking patterns made Feyenoord a formidable side. The club's resurgence under his leadership was a testament to his innovative approach and deep understanding of the game.

Arne Slot's story is a compelling one, marked by a seamless transition from player to coach and characterized by a deep-rooted passion for football. His journey serves as an inspiration to many aspiring coaches, illustrating the importance of learning, adaptability, and a relentless pursuit of excellence. Slot's strategic mind and dedication to the sport continue to leave a lasting impact on Dutch and European football, as he paves the way for future generations of coaches and players.

For more detailed information on Arne Slot's career and influence, you can explore profiles and interviews on platforms such as The Athletic, ESPN, and football databases like Transfermarkt. These sources provide in-depth insights into his coaching philosophy, career milestones, and the transformative impact he has had on the teams he has managed .

As Arne Slot progressed in his career, he became a symbol of what meticulous planning and an innovative approach to football management could achieve. His tenure as head coach at Feyenoord epitomized his deep understanding of the game and his knack for transforming teams into cohesive, high-performing units. His arrival at Feyenoord in 2021 marked a turning point for the club, which had been struggling to regain its former glory in Dutch football.

Slot's coaching philosophy at Feyenoord emphasized fluid, attacking football, underpinned by a solid defensive structure. He quickly established a culture of discipline and unity within the squad, ensuring that every player understood their role and responsibilities on the pitch. His methods were not only focused on physical training but also on enhancing the players' mental and tactical awareness. Under Slot, Feyenoord developed a style of play that combined traditional Dutch values of possession and technical ability with modern principles of pressing and rapid transitions.

One of the most significant aspects of Slot's management at Feyenoord was his ability to develop young talent. The Eredivisie, known for its emphasis on youth development, proved to be an ideal environment for Slot's vision. He nurtured a new generation of players, instilling in them the confidence and tactical intelligence needed to compete at the highest level. His commitment to youth development not only strengthened the squad but also ensured a sustainable future for the club.

In addition to his success in the domestic league, Slot led Feyenoord on a memorable European campaign. His tactical acumen and ability to adapt to different opponents were evident as the team navigated through challenging fixtures against some of Europe's most formidable sides. The international stage provided an opportunity for Slot to showcase his coaching prowess to a wider audience, further establishing his reputation as one of the most promising young managers in football.

Slot's influence extended beyond his tactics and game management. His leadership style fostered a strong sense of camaraderie and mutual respect among the players. He was known for being approachable yet firm, striking a perfect balance between being a mentor and a disciplinarian. His approach created an environment where players could thrive, pushing each other to reach new heights while maintaining a shared commitment to the club's goals.

Another cornerstone of Slot's philosophy was his analytical approach to football. He made extensive use of data and video analysis to prepare his team for matches, a practice that had become increasingly common in modern football. However, Slot distinguished himself by seamlessly integrating these technological advancements into his coaching methods. He was able to simplify complex tactical concepts, making them accessible to his players, and used data to fine-tune their performances. This blend of old-school coaching instincts and modern analysis was crucial to Feyenoord's resurgence under his leadership.

In summary, Arne Slot's journey from a young boy playing football in the streets of Bergentheim to one of the most respected coaches in the Dutch Eredivisie is a testament to his love for the sport, his commitment to continuous learning, and his innovative approach to management. His impact on the teams he has coached, particularly at Feyenoord, continues to resonate, with his tactical strategies and emphasis on youth development serving as a blueprint for success. As his career continues to evolve, Slot remains a pivotal figure in shaping the future of football, both in the Netherlands and beyondd insights into Arne Slot's tactics and philosophy, or if you're curious about his latest achievements, you can explore resources on sports analysis websites or visit official Feyenoord reports .

Arne Slot's youth career and the values that influenced his later approach to the game were defined by the modest and hard-working community of Bergentheim in the Netherlands, where he was born in 1978. From an early age, Slot was immersed in a culture that celebrated teamwork, perseverance, and a passion for football. Growing up in a small village, he played in local youth clubs, where the emphasis was on building a love for the sport rather than achieving early stardom. This experience instilled in him a strong sense of community and humility, qualities that would become central to his managerial philosophy.

Slot's early footballing journey began at his local club, VV Bergentheim, where he honed the basics of his game. At VV Bergentheim, he learned the importance of discipline and hard work. The club's training regime was structured to teach young players how to approach football with a sense of responsibility and dedication. This grassroots environment emphasized skill development, mutual support, and understanding the fundamentals of the game, which had a lasting impact on Slot's tactical perspective.

As Slot progressed through the youth ranks, he showed not only technical proficiency but also a deep understanding of the game, earning a reputation for being a player who thought several moves ahead. His early exposure to playing in multiple positions helped him develop tactical flexibility, an attribute that became a hallmark of his coaching. Slot was influenced by coaches who believed in an attacking, possession-based style of football, as well as by the Dutch "Total Football" philosophy that prioritizes fluidity, player versatility, and spatial awareness. This foundational principle of Total Football inspired Slot to focus on tactics that emphasized team cohesion and strategic ball control.

The influence of Dutch footballing greats like Johan Cruyff and his emphasis on the interdependence of all players on the field was evident even in Slot's youth career. He admired the way Dutch teams managed transitions between defense and attack and how every player had a role in the overall structure. Slot's understanding of this system grew from his time spent learning the intricacies of the game, both on the training pitch and in the classroom. The lessons learned from these experiences instilled a vision that balanced tactical discipline with creative freedom, which would become essential to his coaching methods.

When Slot transitioned from amateur football to the professional level, his dedication and adaptability caught the attention of FC Zwolle (now PEC Zwolle), where he began his professional career in the late 1990s. At Zwolle, he experienced firsthand the challenges of professional football, which solidified his resolve to study the game in more detail. Even as a player, Slot had a reputation for being studious, often analyzing match tactics and exploring ways to outsmart opponents. His time at Zwolle and subsequent clubs, such as NAC Breda and Sparta Rotterdam, further broadened his understanding of football's strategic dimensions and taught him the importance of adaptability in different team setups.

These foundational values—hard work, adaptability, tactical acumen, and an appreciation for the collective effort of the team—shaped Slot's vision for how football should be played and coached. As he transitioned from player to coach, he carried these principles into his managerial career, emphasizing that success comes from a combination of strategic thinking, disciplined execution, and the development of young talent. His upbringing and youth experiences laid the groundwork for his philosophy, combining traditional Dutch footballing principles with modern innovations to create dynamic and cohesive teams.

Slot's youth career and early professional experiences provided him with a comprehensive understanding of how to build a cohesive and adaptive team. The Dutch football landscape was essential in shaping his tactical approach, specifically the principles embedded in the philosophy of "Total Football." The emphasis on fluidity, positioning, and player roles remained a key aspect of how Slot would later construct his teams.

During his years at FC Zwolle, he refined his understanding of the importance of balance in both attack and defense. The Dutch lower leagues were known for being highly competitive and often served as a proving ground for players and future coaches like Slot. Facing various tactical setups and competitive environments, he learned to adapt quickly. His time at NAC Breda and Sparta Rotterdam exposed him to different managerial styles and strategic adjustments that influenced his analytical perspective. For instance, while playing under managers who experimented with innovative formations, Slot developed a keen eye for strategic flexibility.

Despite being a professional player, Slot's dedication to understanding the mechanics of coaching was evident. He often stayed back to engage in post-training discussions with coaches and senior staff. This curiosity about football strategies, formations, and player psychology would later become the foundation of his coaching techniques. Former teammates recall how Slot would analyze match footage and discuss tactical variations, even taking notes about what he learned, demonstrating an early passion for the analytical side of the sport.

Another major influence on Slot was the Dutch emphasis on youth development and player education. As a coach, he would later draw upon these experiences to empower young players, helping them understand their roles in a broader tactical setup. He believed that players who were well-educated in tactical nuances were more adaptable and capable of contributing effectively to the team's success. This belief in continuous learning and adaptation is a value he reinforced in his coaching, a direct result of the experiences and observations he made during his own youth and playing career.

Slot's understanding of football extended beyond tactics to player management. He realized the value of communication and empathy, principles he picked up during the early stages of his career. Building a cohesive locker room environment and fostering trust among players were essential components of his later managerial success. His approach to leadership was not only about giving instructions but also about listening to and understanding the perspectives of his players. This ability to connect on a human level made him a respected figure in the football community, even before his breakthrough as a coach.

Moreover, Slot's progression from a player to a coach allowed him to seamlessly transition his understanding of game dynamics into a managerial role. He understood the physical and psychological demands placed on players and could therefore tailor his training sessions to optimize performance while minimizing burnout. His holistic approach to football management was rooted in his practical experiences on the pitch, where he learned that success required a harmonious blend of strategy, adaptability, and respect for the game.

These experiences during his youth and playing career laid the foundation for his future coaching philosophy, which focused on creating balanced, well-prepared, and tactically flexible teams. Slot's emphasis on education, analysis, and adaptability became trademarks of his managerial style, propelling him into the spotlight as one of the Netherlands' most promising football minds. As he transitioned to a coaching career, these foundational values continued to guide his approach, setting him apart in a highly competitive field.

◇◇◇◇

Arne Slot's playing career took him through several key stages in Dutch football, establishing his reputation as a talented midfielder. His professional journey began at FC Zwolle (later known as PEC Zwolle), where he made a significant impact. Starting in 1995, Slot spent the early years of his career developing his skills with the club, making over 150 appearances and contributing 50 goals in total. His first major achievement with Zwolle came in 2002 when he helped the team win the Eerste Divisie, the second-tier league in the Netherlands.

After his initial success, Slot moved to NAC Breda in 2002, where he continued to hone his craft. At Breda, he became a crucial part of the midfield, helping the team secure multiple seasons in the Eredivisie. Slot played in over 140 league matches and scored 21 goals, solidifying his reputation in the top tier of Dutch football.

In 2007, Slot's career took him to Sparta Rotterdam, where he played for a brief period, contributing six goals in 54 appearances. His time there was short-lived, but Slot continued to make an impression. He returned to PEC Zwolle on loan in 2009, a move that reconnected him with his roots. During this period, he played 28 matches and scored seven goals, once again demonstrating his consistency and ability to control the midfield.

Slot's playing career culminated with his return to PEC Zwolle in 2010, where he finished his professional playing career. He made 74 appearances and scored 16 goals, continuing to be an influential presence in the team's midfield until his retirement.

Throughout his playing career, Slot was known for his technical skill, vision, and tactical intelligence. His ability to read the game and his leadership on the field were evident, and these qualities would later serve him well in his coaching career.

Arne Slot's playing career was marked by his deep understanding of the game and his versatile midfield skills. His technical abilities and vision helped him stand out in the Dutch league, especially at his time with clubs such as PEC Zwolle, NAC Breda, and Sparta Rotterdam. His experience across various teams shaped his tactical approach to football, influencing the way he later led his teams as a coach.

While Slot enjoyed a productive career, it was his leadership and tactical intelligence on the field that garnered attention. Playing in a midfield role, he was often tasked with controlling the tempo of the game, utilizing his ability to make precise passes and read the play. These skills were evident in his long tenure at PEC Zwolle, where he became a fixture in the team's starting XI and helped guide the club to its successes.

Slot's technical qualities, along with his ability to adapt to different tactical systems, made him a respected figure in Dutch football. However, his playing career ended relatively early due to injuries, and he transitioned to coaching, where he applied the principles he had learned throughout his time on the field.

His career at PEC Zwolle, in particular, allowed Slot to make a lasting impact. After a series of successful seasons with the club, he retired from professional football in 2010. This marked the end of his time as a player but laid the groundwork for his later coaching career, where his experiences as a midfielder influenced his coaching style,

emphasizing possession-based football and team discipline
.

Slot's playing career was foundational in shaping the qualities he would later instill in his teams as a coach: tactical awareness, leadership, and a strong understanding of the game's rhythm.

Arne Slot's playing career, though relatively short due to injury, played a pivotal role in shaping his coaching philosophy. After his time with PEC Zwolle, he moved on to NAC Breda, where he gained valuable experience in the top tier of Dutch football. This exposure to higher competition and different tactical approaches contributed to his understanding of football's complexities.

Slot's tactical intelligence was his greatest asset on the field, and it laid the foundation for his approach as a coach. His time at Sparta Rotterdam, where he played the final years of his playing career, was crucial. At Sparta, he honed his leadership skills, adapting to different tactical setups while remaining focused on the core principles of team structure and discipline. His technical abilities, particularly his passing range and vision, enabled him to control matches in the midfield, making him a reliable asset to his teams.

Despite his success as a player, Slot's career was cut short by recurring injuries. He retired from professional football at the relatively young age of 30. However, these early setbacks did not deter him; instead, they became a driving force in his transition to coaching. Understanding the game from both a tactical and a player's perspective provided Slot with a unique insight into what is required to succeed on the pitch.

The values that defined Slot as a player—commitment to team discipline, an emphasis on positional awareness, and a strong understanding of football strategy—became the foundation of his coaching philosophy. These values would later help him lead teams to success, first at AZ Alkmaar, and eventually at Feyenoord, where his tactical innovations were a direct extension of his experiences as a player different playing styles and environments was one of the key features of his playing career. This adaptability, along with his leadership qualities, made him a respected figure in the Dutch football community. His experiences as a player in various teams, where he learned to adjust to different coaching methods, proved invaluable in his later work as a coach, enabling him to understand the needs of players from all backgrounds and playing styles.

Overall, Slot's playing career may not have been extensive, but it was filled with invaluable lessons that have influenced the way he approaches coaching. His experiences, both positive and negative, played a crucial role in shaping his view on football, which would later contribute significantly to his success as one of the most respected young coaches in European football.

Arne Slot's playing career as a midfielder significantly influenced his later coaching philosophy, particularly in areas such as positional play, tactical discipline, and the importance of building from the midfield. Several key experiences during his playing years played a major role in shaping the principles that would define his managerial approach:

1. Positional Intelligence and Tactical Awareness

As a midfielder, Slot's ability to read the game and position himself effectively was crucial. In the modern game, midfielders are often the engine of the team, responsible for linking defense and attack. Slot's intelligence in positioning and anticipating the movement of the ball and opponents gave him an edge. He learned to control the tempo of a match by making the right decisions in terms of positioning, timing, and passing range.

This emphasis on tactical awareness was a trait that Slot later integrated into his coaching. For instance, Slot's possession-based style at Feyenoord is a direct reflection of his understanding of how important it is to control the game through the midfield. He encourages players to focus on positioning and timing to break down opposition defenses, much like a midfielder would in the past.

2. Importance of Passing and Ball Retention

One of the most fundamental roles of a midfielder is to retain possession and distribute the ball accurately, often under pressure. Slot's ability to execute short and long passes allowed him to dictate play. His vision and technique meant that he could break opposition lines and provide support to both defensive and attacking players.

This aspect of his game was instrumental in Slot's evolution as a coach.

In his managerial career, Slot has emphasized ball retention and quick transitions. His focus on high pressing and regaining possession in advanced areas reflects his belief that control of the ball leads to dominance in a match. His coaching style encourages players to be comfortable on the ball and make incisive passes that can unlock defensive structures, echoing his midfield experiences.

3. Linking Attack and Defense

Slot's role as a midfielder required him to serve as the link between attack and defense, understanding the need for balance in all phases of play. Midfielders must be aware of both defensive duties and attacking runs. This ability to transition between defensive and attacking phases seamlessly was something that Slot mastered over his playing career.

In his coaching, Slot's systems often involve a well-organized defense that quickly transitions into attack. At Feyenoord, for example, Slot built a team that balances defensive solidity with an explosive attacking style. His midfielders are expected to press high, recover the ball quickly, and then immediately use the ball to create scoring opportunities. This tactical fluidity is something that Slot learned firsthand in his own playing days.

4. Leadership and Influence on the Field

As a midfielder, Slot was not only involved in the tactical aspects of the game but also in its psychological elements. Midfielders are often the on-field leaders who communicate constantly with their teammates, providing direction and motivation. Slot's experiences as a captain at various clubs, including Sparta Rotterdam, gave him insight into how to manage personalities and control the tempo of a game, especially in difficult moments.

This leadership quality became a cornerstone of his managerial style. Slot is known for his ability to inspire and motivate his players, fostering a sense of unity within the team. He encourages open communication and a collective mentality, which stems from his understanding of how a midfielder must operate as the team's central figure.

5. Dealing with Adversity

Slot's playing career was not without setbacks. He faced injuries that eventually cut short his career. However, these experiences only strengthened his resolve and ability to handle adversity. Slot learned how to adapt to challenging situations, not just as a player but also in terms of maintaining morale within the squad. This resilience became a key attribute that he later instilled in his teams as a coach.

In his coaching career, Slot is known for his resilience in the face of tough situations. Whether dealing with tough losses or challenging opposition, Slot emphasizes the importance of maintaining composure and focus. His ability to stay calm and strategize during difficult moments is a direct result of the adversity he faced during his playing days.

6. The Influence of Playing Under Various Coaches

Throughout his playing career, Slot had the opportunity to play under various coaches, each with their own tactical approaches. This exposure to different coaching styles significantly shaped his understanding of the game. For example, Slot was influenced by the attacking philosophies of coaches in the Dutch league, as well as the importance of team discipline and structure. He learned the value of positional play and quick transitions from these experiences.

As a coach, Slot blends various philosophies, adapting elements he learned from his playing days. His work at AZ Alkmaar and Feyenoord reflects his ability to draw from different coaching methods and implement them in a way that suits his teams' strengths. His tactical flexibility, honed from his experiences under various coaches, is now a hallmark of his coaching philosophy.

Conclusion

Arne Slot's experiences as a midfielder—his tactical awareness, passing ability, leadership qualities, and resilience—have been central to shaping his coaching career. These formative years, combined with his exposure to different tactical systems, have made Slot a versatile and strategic coach. His emphasis on possession, high pressing, and intelligent transitions on the field are direct reflections of the lessons he learned as a player. Today, Slot's philosophy continues to evolve, but it remains deeply rooted in his experiences as a player in the heart of the midfield.

◇◇◇◇

Arne Slot's transition from player to coach is a pivotal moment in his career, shaped by his deep understanding of football and a strong desire to improve the game. After retiring as a player, Slot initially joined PEC Zwolle as an assistant coach, which laid the foundation for his future coaching journey. His decision to switch to coaching came with challenges, primarily due to his relatively modest playing career, which was not particularly high-profile. However, he was determined to use his tactical acumen and passion for the sport to build a successful coaching career.

Slot faced several challenges as a rookie coach, particularly in navigating the pressures of working with professional athletes and managing expectations. His approach was analytical, often stopping training sessions to emphasize precision, which was initially met with some resistance from players. However, this high-standard coaching approach paid off in the long run, as his former players later acknowledged that these moments shaped their growth as footballers.

His transition was significantly influenced by his experiences with innovative coaching techniques. Slot was known for experimenting with new technology, like drone-assisted filming, to analyze team performance from multiple angles. This unique blend of traditional tactical strategies and modern tools helped distinguish his coaching philosophy. Slot's attention to detail, his focus on technical and tactical development, and his insistence on perfection created a solid framework for success.

One of the defining features of Slot's coaching philosophy is his emphasis on holistic development, not just on-field performance. At PEC Zwolle, he integrated academic success into his football program, underscoring the importance of balance in young players' lives. This educational focus not only nurtured better footballers but well-rounded individuals, a principle he carried into his later roles, including his time at Feyenoord, where he revitalized the team with an attacking style and helped develop key players.

Despite early setbacks, including being sacked at AZ after a strong start, Slot's resilience and innovative thinking led to impressive successes, such as leading Feyenoord to the 2022 UEFA Europa Conference League final and the Eredivisie title in 2023. His tenure at Feyenoord solidified his reputation as one of the brightest coaching talents in European football.

Arne Slot's transition into coaching was marked by determination and a willingness to adapt. After his playing career, Slot took his first significant step in coaching at PEC Zwolle, where he started as an assistant coach before stepping into managerial roles. His journey was not without challenges. Despite not having the high-profile career of some of his peers, Slot's deep tactical understanding of the game allowed him to make an impact quickly, though it was not an easy transition. He had to build trust with both players and management, and it took time for his ideas to gain traction.

One of the key aspects of Slot's coaching development was his commitment to detail and innovative thinking. He was a firm believer in the power of data, technology, and video analysis. In a world where most teams relied heavily on traditional coaching methods, Slot embraced tools like drone technology to get an aerial view of his team's movement and strategy during training sessions. This attention to detail and the use of modern technology to assess and improve his team's performance were among the reasons his approach stood out.

Slot's philosophy was rooted in his own playing experiences, where he focused on discipline, technique, and tactical awareness. He drew inspiration from the more experienced coaches he worked under, including the tactical insight of Dick Advocaat, but Slot's vision was always his own. He took lessons from his time playing for clubs like Sparta Rotterdam and PEC Zwolle, where he often operated as a midfielder. It was from these experiences that he learned the importance of patience, teamwork, and flexibility, principles that he instilled in his coaching methods.

At AZ Alkmaar, where he worked before his current role at Feyenoord, Slot's reputation grew significantly. Despite an early setback with his departure from AZ, Slot demonstrated resilience, bouncing back with a more refined approach. His tactical nous, commitment to attacking football, and ability to develop young talent came to the forefront. His work with young players at AZ set the stage for his future success at Feyenoord, where his tactical mastery and ability to inspire players reached new heights. Feyenoord thrived under his leadership, showcasing an exciting brand of football that led them to their first Eredivisie title in 2023ability to transition into a head coach role successfully was a product of both his playing career and his unyielding commitment to evolving as a manager. It wasn't just about coaching a team—it was about creating a footballing philosophy that could be implemented long-term. His strategic choices, reliance on technology, and dedication to youth development have set him apart as one of the top managers in the Eredivisie. Through his career trajectory, Slot demonstrated that with hard work, self-belief, and an innovative approach, the challenges faced by new coaches can be overcome.

Arne Slot's transition from player to coach also involved navigating the practical realities of coaching, including managing player egos, dealing with media pressure, and developing a network of trusted assistants. Early in his career, Slot had to reconcile his passion for tactical innovation with the need to maintain the morale of the squad. His ability to stay calm under pressure and his methodical approach to problem-solving became essential as he learned the nuances of leadership from the touchline.

One of the major hurdles Slot faced in his early coaching years was establishing credibility, given his relative inexperience compared to some other high-profile coaches in the Eredivisie. However, his success at clubs like AZ Alkmaar helped him build a reputation for understanding the game on a deeper level. Slot's playing background, especially his experience in midfield, had instilled a nuanced understanding of the game that made his coaching approach distinct. His ability to read the game and implement tactical changes quickly, something he had done as a player, became even more valuable as a coach. It allowed him to make well-informed decisions that sometimes led to tactical masterstrokes that set his teams apartr, Slot's focus on the development of younger players became a hallmark of his coaching style. At AZ Alkmaar, he took pride in cultivating youth talent and integrating them into the first team. His faith in younger players helped the club become known for its ability to produce top-quality footballers, many of whom went on to have successful careers in both the Eredivisie and abroad. This dedication to youth development was one of the key pillars of Slot's philosophy, helping ensure that his coaching career would be sustainable in the long term. This commitment to developing players, rather than just relying on established stars, would be a cornerstone of his later success at Feyenoord 【69†sourcerd's appointment of Arne Slot marked a significant turning point in his career. As a coach with a clear tactical identity, Slot was entrusted with the responsibility of guiding Feyenoord back to the top of Dutch football. The challenges were formidable— Feyenoord had a rich history, but had seen less success in recent years. Slot's arrival coincided with a period of rebuilding at the club, and his focus on building a cohesive team and implementing a dynamic, attacking style of play soon began to yield results .

In man early coaching challenges shaped the tactical flexibility that became a defining characteristic of his style. Slot understood that football was an ever-evolving game, and that as a coach, he needed to evolve too. His tactical acumen, combined with his work ethic and ability to inspire his players, ensured that he would make a significant impact on whichever club he managed. By focusing on creating an organized, yet fluid, attacking team, Slot made his mark as a coach capable of inspiring both young talent and seasoned professionals 【69†source】 .

In sum's transition to coaching was not without its challenges, but his understanding of the game, his commitment to tactical innovation, and his emphasis on youth development allowed him to carve out a successful managerial career. These early experiences, from managing squads with mixed experience to his reliance on tactical discipline and youth, laid the groundwork for his future achievements. His ability to build teams that were not only competitive but also exciting to watch, solidified his place as one of the most respected coaches in Dutch football.

Arne Slot's transition to coaching was influenced by both his playing career and his evolving understanding of football tactics. After ending his playing days, Slot initially took on a coaching role with the youth team at FC Utrecht. This was an important step, where he began to shape his tactical philosophy under the guidance of various mentors. One key influence during this early coaching period was Erik ten Hag, the former Ajax coach. Slot worked alongside him at FC Utrecht, gaining insight into ten Hag's meticulous approach to football, which focused on building from the back and pressing high. This period provided Slot with the foundational principles that would later shape his own methods as a coach.

Slot's tactical philosophy is rooted in possession-based football with a focus on aggressive pressing and high-intensity play, which he refined through his time at AZ Alkmaar. His teams play an organized, high-pressing style that seeks to recover the ball quickly in the opponent's half. His aggressive approach to pressing is something that became prominent in his work at Feyenoord, where Slot further developed these tactics and integrated them into his team's identity.

His experience with FC Utrecht and AZ was vital in shaping his understanding of football at a deeper tactical level. Slot emphasized the importance of fluid attacking movements, with a well-coordinated system that encouraged wide play while maintaining flexibility in the final third. His philosophy emphasizes offensive transitions, relying on quick passing and coordinated pressing to regain possession swiftly.

These early coaching roles, combined with the mentorship of influential figures like ten Hag, allowed Slot to lay the groundwork for his subsequent success in coaching at the top levels of Dutch football. His ability to develop young talent and implement dynamic, aggressive football tactics would later define his time at Feyenoord, where he earned widespread recognition for both his coaching acumen and his leadership.

Arne Slot's initial steps into coaching involved learning both from the field and from experienced mentors. One of the key figures who shaped his approach early on was Erik ten Hag. At FC Utrecht, Slot observed and worked alongside ten Hag, who was known for his attention to detail, his tactical awareness, and his success in organizing his teams to control possession while maintaining intense pressing. This mentorship laid the groundwork for Slot's own tactical ideology. Ten Hag's influence on Slot was profound, especially regarding the importance of team shape, discipline in pressing, and an organized transition from defense to attack.

Slot's early coaching roles also helped him build a foundation for his managerial career. At FC Utrecht, he moved from a youth coach to managing the first team, which provided a steep learning curve. However, his time at AZ Alkmaar was the breakthrough that truly established him as a promising tactical mind. At AZ, he had the freedom to experiment with his ideas in a top-flight setting, and he implemented a more aggressive high press combined with a focus on quick, direct football. His time at AZ helped him hone his ability to craft fluid, attacking systems that allowed his players to dominate possession and control the tempo of the game.

It was during this period at AZ that Slot's tactical understanding matured significantly, enabling him to blend high pressing with intelligent ball movement. His defensive shape, combined with quick transitions to attack, allowed his teams to maintain pressure on the opposition both defensively and offensively. The principles Slot began to solidify at AZ would become hallmarks of his approach at Feyenoord these early experiences, Slot not only refined his tactical approach but also developed a deeper understanding of how to manage teams, manage players' emotions, and maintain consistency under pressure. These lessons in leadership and tactical flexibility were integral to Slot's later successes at Feyenoord, where his coaching philosophy reached its full expression.

Arne Slot's transition to coaching was deeply shaped by his growing understanding of tactical theory, honed through the mentorship of key figures in Dutch football. His time at FC Utrecht, under Erik ten Hag, gave Slot invaluable exposure to high-level tactical thinking. Ten Hag, known for his meticulous approach, instilled in Slot the importance of pressing, maintaining defensive structure, and the fluidity required for modern football.

Slot's time at AZ Alkmaar marked the start of his journey as a head coach. There, Slot began implementing his tactical ideas, focusing on high pressing and a proactive style of play that revolved around possession. His emphasis on winning the ball back quickly after losing possession became a hallmark of his coaching identity. This aggressive pressing style was refined under his guidance at AZ, and it became the foundation of his future successes.

The development of Slot's coaching philosophy was also influenced by his observations of foreign football. He was particularly drawn to the tactical innovations of teams like Barcelona and Bayern Munich, whose high possession games and attacking transitions provided him with further inspiration. His ability to synthesize ideas from different football cultures and tailor them to his own team's strengths set Slot apart as an adaptable and innovative coach.

By the time he moved to Feyenoord, Slot had a clear vision of how he wanted his teams to play. His foundational years in coaching equipped him with the tools necessary to manage not only the tactical side of the game but also the human aspect—working with players, building trust, and maintaining a competitive edge. His journey from youth coaching to becoming a respected tactical mind in Dutch football showcases his ability to adapt and learn from every environment, gradually molding his own coaching style that would later lead to success at Feyenoord.

Arne Slot's decision to transition from playing to coaching was motivated by a blend of personal ambition, tactical curiosity, and an evolving desire to shape the future of football. After an injury-prone playing career, Slot's drive to continue within the footballing world found its path in coaching. The decision was likely influenced by the tactical appreciation that developed during his time as a player, particularly his deep engagement with the technical aspects of midfield play. As a player, Slot was known for his vision, creativity, and passing accuracy—qualities that naturally lent themselves to coaching, where attention to detail and understanding team dynamics are key.

Slot's first coaching role came with the FC Utrecht U-19 team, where he began to lay the foundation for his coaching philosophy. Here, he took on a mentoring role, guiding young players while also learning about the intricacies of coaching from the senior staff. His move to a more prominent coaching position at AZ Alkmaar marked a significant step in his journey. AZ presented an opportunity for Slot to refine his tactical vision, focusing on a high-pressing, possession-based style of play. This phase of his career saw Slot experimenting with the principles of modern football, influenced by the tactical schools of thought that dominate the European game.

Key to Slot's development were the mentors who helped guide his tactical evolution. One of the most influential figures during this phase was Erik ten Hag, who mentored Slot during his time at FC Utrecht. Ten Hag's approach, marked by disciplined pressing and fluid attacking transitions, shaped Slot's tactical mindset and helped him grasp the importance of flexibility in coaching. Ten Hag, known for his methodical work with Ajax, emphasized the idea of adapting tactical frameworks based on player strengths and weaknesses, a concept Slot would later integrate into his own philosophylkmaar, Slot was able to incorporate elements of these lessons into his coaching. His tactical acumen was enhanced by studying various successful European teams, including Barcelona and Bayern Munich, whose possession-based styles were tailored to Slot's understanding of high-pressing football. This period marked Slot's emergence as a promising young coach with a strong tactical foundation and a focus on attacking football .

In su Slot's early coaching journey was heavily shaped by his mentors, particularly Erik ten Hag, and his exposure to cutting-edge football tactics. His time in youth football and at AZ Alkmaar allowed him to refine his methods, establishing a solid foundation for his later successes at Feyenoord. His decision to become a coach was not only about continuing his career in football but also about nurturing a deeper connection to the game through tactical innovation.

As Arne Slot transitioned into coaching, his path forward was not without challenges. The shift from being a player to a coach often involves a steep learning curve. Players, particularly those who had enjoyed long careers like Slot, often face difficulties when adapting to the tactical and emotional demands of coaching. Slot's initial foray into coaching was marked by his early involvement in youth teams, where he honed his methods and gained experience managing young players. This hands-on approach gave him the opportunity to understand the development process at its most fundamental level, allowing him to shape his ideas about football without the immediate pressure of senior team results.

His transition was also informed by the challenges of finding his own coaching style. While Slot's tactical ideas were initially influenced by mentors like Erik ten Hag, he had to carve out a distinctive identity. His time at FC Utrecht provided essential insight into creating systems of play that emphasized possession and a structured, yet fluid, defensive framework. Slot's development was a gradual process in which he sought to blend tactical discipline with the creative freedom that he had valued as a playerly stages of Slot's coaching career also involved confronting the realities of managing a squad of senior players. Unlike the structured environment of youth teams, coaching first-team professionals involves handling a wide variety of personalities and playing styles. He had to learn how to motivate experienced players, manage egos, and adapt his tactics to meet the immediate needs of a match. One of the first significant tests of his coaching ability came at AZ Alkmaar, where he managed to take the team to an impressive third-place finish in Eredivisie and attract the attention of bigger clubs. His ability to create a cohesive team that performed with intensity and purpose underlined his growing tactical understanding .

As his began to grow, Slot's confidence as a coach increased. He became known for his attacking, possession-oriented style, which contrasted with the defensive pragmatism that characterized many teams in the Eredivisie. His ideas reflected a modern approach to football, one that emphasized fluid transitions, pressing high, and controlling possession. This brand of football was not without its critics, but Slot's teams showed consistency and energy in their matches, which made them exciting to watch. These formative years as a coach were pivotal for Slot, as they allowed him to build the foundation upon which his later success at Feyenoord would be based.

In conclusion, Arne Slot's transition to coaching involved overcoming many challenges, from adjusting to new tactical demands to managing senior players. The guidance he received from mentors like Erik ten Hag was crucial in shaping his philosophy, but Slot's personal journey as a coach helped him refine his own methods. His experiences in youth football and at AZ Alkmaar were formative, setting the stage for his eventual rise as one of the most promising coaches in Dutch football. His early career laid the groundwork for his success, proving that the best coaches are those who understand the game from both a player's and a manager's perspective 【83†source】 .

◇◇◇◇

Arne Slot's time at AZ Alkmaar was marked by a tactical evolution that showcased his ability to implement an attacking, possession-based game while maintaining defensive stability. Slot's influence on the team can be seen through his strategic use of formations and the development of key tactical principles that made AZ a formidable side in Dutch football.

One of Slot's key contributions was his focus on positional play, which sought to stretch the pitch and create numerical advantages in tight spaces. His teams often utilized formations such as the 4-2-3-1 to support a fluid attacking style, with a strong emphasis on building play from the back. Central to this was his use of the double pivot system, where midfielders played crucial roles in both controlling space and transitioning the ball into attack. This allowed players like Idrissi and Stengs to exploit wide areas, while the forwards, including Boadu, were tasked with dropping deeper into midfield to open space and receive passes.

Slot also introduced high pressing strategies, using the attacking players to press the opposition high up the pitch, often forcing mistakes and quick transitions. This was an essential part of his system, as AZ looked to regain possession rapidly and capitalize on any opportunities. In defensive situations, Slot's team maintained a compact shape with their midfielders providing cover, adapting to counter-attacks without losing their structure.

One of the standout features of Slot's tenure at AZ was his ability to generate attacking opportunities through precise movement and rotations in the final third. Players frequently made blind-sided runs or dropped into pockets of space to draw defenders out of position, creating openings for late arrivals or quick combinations. His tactical innovations at AZ Alkmaar laid the groundwork for his later success at Feyenoord, where his strategies evolved and were refined, leading the club to Eredivisie glory.

Slot's coaching at AZ reflected his vision for an engaging, modern style of football—aggressive in attack, organized in defense, and flexible in possession. His approach not only resulted in an impressive league finish but also helped to elevate the quality of play within Dutch football, influencing his later work at Feyenoord.

Arne Slot's impact at AZ Alkmaar was also evident in the way he integrated young players into the first team, demonstrating his belief in developing homegrown talent. His ability to blend experience with youth was pivotal in AZ's success, with players like Myron Boadu, Calvin Stengs, and Owen Wijndal emerging as key figures under his management. Slot fostered a culture of responsibility among his players, where each individual understood their tactical role, but also had the freedom to express themselves within the framework of the team's collective ambition.

Furthermore, Slot's tactical intelligence was evident in his approach to European competition. AZ Alkmaar's style under him was not just about attacking; Slot's teams could adjust to different opposition, using their high pressing and possession-based game to dominate in both domestic and international settings. This adaptability in approach helped AZ perform admirably in European fixtures, showing that Slot could balance attacking flair with defensive discipline to compete at a higher level.

His success at AZ Alkmaar culminated in a thrilling second-place finish in the Eredivisie during the 2019-2020 season, just behind Ajax, with Slot guiding the team to one of its most consistent campaigns in recent years. The style of play he instilled continued to garner praise from pundits, who lauded his ability to make AZ Alkmaar one of the most exciting teams to watch in the league. This period cemented Slot's reputation as one of the brightest managerial talents in Dutch football and set the stage for his subsequent move to Feyenoord, where he would further showcase his tactical brilliance.

Arne Slot's tenure at AZ Alkmaar was marked by a record-breaking performance that firmly established his place among the most innovative coaches in Dutch football. One of the most striking metrics of his success was his impressive points-per-game ratio, which stood as a testament to both his tactical acumen and ability to foster consistency across an entire season. Under his leadership, AZ achieved an extraordinary 2.16 points per game (ppg) in the Eredivisie, a figure that placed Slot in an elite category among the league's modern managers. This record highlights not just his success in domestic competitions, but also his ability to create a sustainable and winning system, even under the pressure of playing against teams like Ajax and PSV Eindhoven, who have historically dominated the league.

Slot's approach to football is often analyzed through the lens of his heavy emphasis on a possession-based style mixed with dynamic pressing. His strategy, while relying heavily on ball retention and a high press, was also versatile enough to counter the strengths of his opponents. This blend of attacking fluidity and tactical discipline allowed AZ Alkmaar to dominate matches both domestically and in European competitions. Slot's teams were often able to sustain possession with sharp, short passes while also pressing high up the pitch, a hallmark of modern Dutch football, reminiscent of the total football philosophy but with a more structured and refined approach.

His tactical philosophy also had a long-term impact on Dutch football. Slot's method of incorporating youth players into the first team, coupled with his tactical sophistication, signaled a new wave of Dutch coaches who are both well-versed in modern football's technical demands and committed to integrating younger talent into the senior squad. Players such as Myron Boadu and Calvin Stengs flourished under his guidance, benefiting from the tactical system that prioritized intelligent movement, versatility, and technical skill. This not only helped AZ become a formidable force in Dutch football but also set a new standard for how young players could thrive in top-flight football by adopting Slot's demanding yet nurturing environment.

In terms of broader influence, Slot's era at AZ Alkmaar encouraged a rethinking of the tactical approaches in Dutch football. The Eredivisie, traditionally known for its attacking flair, saw Slot infuse a more structured yet fluid style of play, one that was not just about possession but about smart transitions, collective movement, and defensive stability. His focus on high pressing and winning back possession quickly added a layer of sophistication to the league's typical attacking mindset. The result was an incredibly high tempo of play, but one that was tactically controlled, with each player understanding their roles clearly both with and without the ball.

The success of Slot at AZ Alkmaar also caught the attention of larger clubs in Europe, cementing his reputation as a coach capable of transforming teams and achieving results against the odds. Slot's point tally with AZ showcased the potential for clubs outside the traditional top-tier powers in the Netherlands to compete effectively in both domestic and international settings. His time at AZ served as a pivotal chapter in the club's history and also acted as a springboard for his eventual transition to Feyenoord, where he would go on to build further on his tactical success and legacy.

In conclusion, Arne Slot's record-breaking points-per-game at AZ Alkmaar highlighted the exceptional quality of his management. His tactical philosophy has had a lasting impact not only on the club but also on Dutch football as a whole, encouraging a new era of coaching that balances technical football with practical and intelligent decision-making. His success with AZ proved that a well-executed tactical plan, rooted in high-pressing football and possession, could lead to sustained success in both league and European competitions. Through his work at AZ, Slot made a significant contribution to shaping the future of Dutch football, influencing how teams approach possession, high pressing, and youth development.

CHAPTER 2

◇◇◇◇

Arne Slot's appointment as Feyenoord's head coach marked a pivotal moment in the club's history, as he sought to rejuvenate the team and return them to the top of Dutch football. Upon his arrival, Slot was tasked with improving a team that had underperformed, and he approached this challenge with clear objectives: to increase competitiveness in the Eredivisie, bring stability, and restore pride at the club.

Slot's first steps involved implementing a tactical philosophy rooted in high pressing, fluid attacking play, and defensive solidity. His 4-2-3-1 formation mirrored his successful strategies at AZ Alkmaar, with significant emphasis on positional play and quick transitions. One of his core strategies was improving ball possession, and he swiftly raised Feyenoord's average possession to over 60% from 52% the season prior. Slot's approach wasn't just about ball retention but also about making quick, purposeful attacks once possession was regained.

The transformation was evident not only in the tactical systems but also in the team's mentality. Slot's leadership fostered a culture of resilience and unity within the squad. He focused on nurturing individual talents while ensuring the team functioned as a cohesive unit. Under his guidance, players like Lutsharel Geertruida and Javairô Dilrosun thrived, and Slot emphasized creativity in the final third, which significantly improved the team's attacking output.

Feyenoord's playing style under Slot became characterized by a dynamic attacking approach. The team's wingers, full-backs, and number 10 players were encouraged to interchange fluidly, creating overloads in wide areas and opening up space for quick crosses or through balls. This led to a higher number of goals scored per match.

Slot also paid attention to defensive structure, ensuring the team maintained balance between offensive freedom and defensive discipline. His defense was compact, with a disciplined press that allowed minimal space for opponents. Even when they dropped deeper, they retained organization, able to press efficiently when opportunities arose.

The results were undeniable: Feyenoord secured an Eredivisie title and consistently impressed in European competitions, achieving victories over top-tier teams. This success demonstrated that Slot's tactics not only revitalized the squad but also made Feyenoord a force to be reckoned with on both domestic and international stages.

Arne Slot's tenure at Feyenoord represents a transformative period for the club, both tactically and culturally. His appointment as head coach provided the catalyst for a resurgence, as he inherited a team with great potential but in need of structure and guidance. Slot's vision for the team involved more than just improving results; it was about establishing a modern, fluid playing style while ensuring consistency and stability, particularly in the Eredivisie.

Slot's tactical approach emphasized high pressing, a balanced defense, and quick transitions, similar to the successful strategies he used at AZ Alkmaar. His implementation of a 4-2-3-1 formation allowed for a dynamic attacking setup that relied on possession and fluid interchanges between the forwards and midfielders. This tactical structure was not only designed to create overloads and exploit space in wide areas but also ensured that the team maintained defensive discipline when the ball was lost. By introducing a high pressing game, Slot's Feyenoord was able to recover the ball quickly and push forward rapidly, which translated into increased goals scored and more attacking opportunities.

The statistical improvements under Slot were evident. Feyenoord's possession increased to over 60%, a significant rise from the 52% the team averaged before his arrival. This elevated ball control allowed for greater dominance in matches, enabling the team to dictate the tempo and control the flow of the game. Moreover, Slot's tactical adjustments led to a more expansive attacking strategy. The movement of players, particularly in the final third, was more fluid, and this improved coordination resulted in more goals and better overall team performance.

Player development also played a crucial role in Slot's success. By focusing on individual players while fostering a team-oriented mentality, Slot was able to draw out the best from talents like Lutsharel Geertruida and Javairô Dilrosun, whose contributions were key to the team's resurgence. This focus on development, alongside tactical evolution, helped Slot improve the overall quality of the team and foster a winning mentality.

In conclusion, Slot's first years at Feyenoord not only yielded a league title but also a long-term foundation for sustained success. His tactical acumen and focus on player development revitalized the club and restored its competitive edge, making Feyenoord a dominant force in Dutch football once more.

◇◇◇◇

Arne Slot's tactical philosophy is rooted in a high-pressing, possession-based style that focuses on ball retention, quick transitions, and creating overloads in wide and central areas. His approach to football combines elements of modern tactical trends with a clear strategic framework that aims to dominate both the ball and the opposition in key phases of the game.

High-Pressing System

A defining feature of Slot's philosophy is his high pressing game, which is essential in regaining possession quickly after losing the ball. This tactic requires the players to press aggressively in advanced positions, forcing opponents to make mistakes in their own half. Slot encourages his players to press collectively, with the aim of compressing the pitch and denying space to the opposition. The pressing triggers are often linked to the positioning of key players: the forwards and attacking midfielders press from the front, while the full-backs and central midfielders form compact lines to ensure the pressing is synchronized.

This type of pressing system places a great demand on fitness and understanding between players, as they must operate as a cohesive unit. In this system, the full-backs play a critical role in ensuring the team stays compact and helps in pressing higher up the pitch, while the midfielders act as the pressure conduits. By forcing the opposition into areas where they are uncomfortable, Slot creates opportunities to win the ball high up the pitch and launch rapid counter-attacks.

Possession-Based Play

In addition to high pressing, Slot is a staunch advocate of possession-based football. He believes in controlling the tempo of the game by keeping the ball in the team's possession for long spells. This does not just mean dominating in terms of percentage, but actively looking for ways to break down the opposition through intelligent passing sequences and movement. The emphasis is on fluid ball circulation, quick interchanges, and positional rotations to stretch the opposition and create gaps for attacking players to exploit.

At Feyenoord, Slot has been able to implement a possession-heavy game in a way that maximizes the attacking potential of his players. His teams are built around a solid passing foundation, with the centre-backs and midfielders being the main architects of the build-up play. Full-backs are often involved in attacking sequences, contributing both width and support in the final third. The focus is not just on keeping possession for the sake of it, but on using it as a tool to draw opponents out of position and create chancesns

One of the hallmarks of Slot's tactical system is the emphasis on quick transitions, particularly when the team regains possession. After a successful press or interception, Slot encourages his team to transition rapidly from defense to attack. This quick change of pace catches the opposition off guard, exploiting moments when they are disorganized. Slot's team is adept at playing quick, vertical passes that switch the ball from the defensive third to the attacking third within seconds.

The emphasis on transitions is particularly evident in Slot's use of dynamic forwards and wingers who can stretch the defense and create immediate attacking threats. Players like Feyenoord's Arne Slot have been key in Slot's setup because of their ability to create space quickly and exploit counter-attacking situations. Slot ensures that once his team regains the ball, it's almost immediately turned into an offensive opportunity .

Fluid Attack t's attacking philosophy is based on fluidity and positional play. He often sets up his team in a way that allows attackers to drift between the lines, create overloads, and open space for others. His attackers are highly mobile, with an emphasis on understanding spatial dynamics and exploiting weaknesses in opposition defenses. This fluidity in attack allows Feyenoord to constantly change formations depending on the situation, whether they need width, depth, or numerical superiority in certain areas of the pitch.

The movement in Slot's attacking setup is highly coordinated. The front players are often tasked with interchanging positions, drawing defenders out of place to create space for runners from deep positions. The midfielders are integral in linking up play and ensuring the team maintains control and balance throughout the match. In possession, Slot's side often looks to overload key areas of the field, both to dictate the tempo and to increase the likelihood of creating a numerical advantage .

Defensive Solidity and Structure

Wdoubtedly attacking in its approach, it also places a strong emphasis on defensive solidity. The high press serves to limit the opposition's time on the ball, but Slot also ensures that his team has a structured defensive shape when they are not in possession. This includes maintaining a compact formation when defending deep and ensuring that the defensive midfielders are well-positioned to intercept passes or provide cover for the central defenders.

One key aspect of Slot's defensive approach is his emphasis on teamwork. Each player, from the forwards to the full-backs, has a clear understanding of their defensive duties. The team works together to close down spaces and restrict the opposition's attacking options. This is achieved by a combination of individual pressing triggers and collective responsibility for tracking runners and intercepting passes .

In summary, Arne Slot's tactical philosophy isated blend of high pressing, possession-based play, and quick transitions. His approach prioritizes not only attacking fluidity but also ensures defensive organization. The success of this system is visible in both the performances of his teams and the statistical improvements in ball possession, goals scored, and defensive stability. Slot's adaptability to both the tactical demands of the Eredivisie and his ability to implement these strategies at Feyenoord demonstrate his growth as a coach and his deep understanding of modern football dynamics. As his career continues to evolve, his tactical system remains at the forefront of his coaching ethos, making him one of the most innovative managers in Dutch football.

Arne Slot is known for his preference for a flexible, attacking style of football that focuses on exploiting the opposition's weaknesses while maintaining control of the game. His approach is based on high possession, quick transitions, and fluid attacking movements, all aimed at creating goal-scoring opportunities while being adaptable to changing circumstances during matches. Slot trains his teams to execute this style through a combination of structured drills, tactical exercises, and player autonomy in understanding the flow of the game.

Flexibility and Fluidity

One of Slot's key beliefs is that football should be played with fluidity and flexibility, adapting to the circumstances of each match. This flexibility is seen in his tactical setup, where his teams can seamlessly shift formations based on the context of the game. For example, while Slot typically employs a 4-3-3 system, his teams are trained to move between various shapes, such as a 3-4-3 or 4-2-3-1, depending on whether they are attacking or defending. This adaptability helps the team respond dynamically to different styles of opposition.

In terms of attacking play, Slot's philosophy emphasizes creating overloads in key areas of the pitch—particularly wide areas and central zones. His wingers are encouraged to cut inside, while full-backs provide the width, allowing the attacking midfielder or center-forward to exploit spaces. Slot encourages his players to read the game and make intelligent runs, ensuring that when the ball moves from one player to another, the opposition is constantly forced into defensive adjustments.

Attacking Play and Possession

In Slot's system, possession is not just about keeping the ball for the sake of it; it's about controlling the tempo and dictating the play. Slot trains his players to move the ball quickly and purposefully, creating opportunities for incisive passes through the opposition's defensive lines. This requires not only a high level of technical ability but also an understanding of how to manipulate space and time during the game.

Slot's players are drilled to make quick, precise passes that move the ball forward, rather than backward. Central midfielders, who are crucial to this aspect of Slot's philosophy, are expected to be comfortable with both short, quick passes and longer through balls to break defensive lines. Slot uses drills that emphasize ball movement under pressure, teaching players to maintain composure and find solutions even when faced with tight opposition marks.

Transition Play

Another hallmark of Slot's attacking philosophy is his emphasis on quick transitions. When his team wins possession, they immediately shift to attack, using speed and precision to capitalize on disorganized defenses. Slot's attacking players are trained to move rapidly and make intelligent runs that stretch the opposition and create spaces in the final third.

This quick transition play requires a high level of physical conditioning, as players need to switch from defensive to offensive roles within seconds of regaining the ball. Slot focuses on building a cohesive team where everyone is aware of their responsibilities, whether they are pressing high or making runs during transitions. The forwards, in particular, are given specific drills to work on timing their movements, while midfielders are encouraged to play quick, incisive passes to exploit the spaces left by the opposition.

Player Development and Tactical Understanding

One of the most important elements of Slot's training methodology is his focus on individual player development, especially when it comes to tactical understanding. Slot places a strong emphasis on educating his players about positional play and their roles in the system, ensuring that they understand when to be fluid and when to stick to the plan. His teams are drilled to recognize patterns in the game and react accordingly.

For example, Slot works closely with his full-backs to ensure that they are not just defensively solid but also capable of contributing to the attack. They are trained to push up the pitch, supporting wingers and midfielders in offensive movements. At the same time, Slot ensures that the center-backs and midfielders are able to cover for the advancing full-backs, maintaining the defensive integrity of the team.

The Importance of Communication and Understanding

Slot's attacking game also relies heavily on strong communication and understanding between players. He places a premium on players being able to talk to each other on the pitch, directing and organizing each other's movements, especially during transitions and high-pressing situations. Training sessions are designed to foster this communication, often using small-sided games and tactical drills where players must constantly communicate their positions and intentions.

In many respects, Slot's success lies in his ability to blend tactical discipline with creative freedom. His teams are well-drilled in positional play and structure, but they also have the freedom to improvise within that framework. This balance of discipline and creativity allows his players to make the most of attacking opportunities while maintaining the team's overall shape and defensive stability.

Conclusion

Arne Slot's preference for a flexible, attacking style of football is built on a foundation of possession, rapid transitions, and tactical understanding. His training methods emphasize the importance of individual player development, with a strong focus on team cohesion and communication. Slot's approach is effective because it allows his teams to adjust to different in-game situations, while still maintaining a coherent, attacking philosophy. As Slot continues to evolve as a coach, his emphasis on attacking football, combined with a tactical discipline, is likely to keep him at the forefront of modern coaching.

◇◇◇◇

Arne Slot's coaching philosophy is not just about tactical innovation and technical ability; it also heavily emphasizes the mental toughness of his players. Slot understands that to succeed at the highest level, players need to cultivate resilience, both on and off the pitch. Mental resilience is crucial for navigating the highs and lows of football, especially in high-pressure situations that can make or break a season.

The Role of Mental Toughness in Slot's Philosophy

Mental resilience is at the core of Slot's player development approach. He believes that a football team cannot thrive based solely on physical ability and technical skills. Players must also be able to cope with adversity, remain focused under pressure, and respond positively to setbacks. In his experience, football matches often come down to mental fortitude rather than physical superiority. As Slot himself has expressed, "Football is not just a game of tactics; it's a game of decisions, under pressure, and the ability to stay calm when it matters most."

Training the Mind: The Importance of Psychological Preparedness

Slot works closely with his players to ensure they are psychologically prepared for both the challenges they face on the pitch and the demands of professional football. One of his key methods for developing mental resilience is through tactical drills that simulate game-like pressure. For example, during training sessions, Slot will often create scenarios where players must make decisions quickly while under physical pressure. This not only helps with technical and tactical decision-making but also with staying calm in stressful situations.

In addition to tactical drills, Slot uses psychological exercises to help players manage their emotions, especially when they are facing challenges such as being behind in a game or dealing with criticism from the media. He encourages open communication among the squad and emphasizes the importance of supporting each other, especially in tough moments. This is evident in his approach to dealing with losing streaks or poor performances—Slot works hard to keep morale high and encourages a mentality where players focus on improving rather than dwelling on past mistakes.

The Power of Positivity

A key component of Slot's approach to building mental toughness is fostering a positive and growth-oriented mindset within the team. He encourages his players to focus on solutions rather than problems, a mindset that he believes is essential for overcoming setbacks. In post-match debriefs, Slot often emphasizes what went right during the game rather than dwelling too much on the mistakes made. This helps players understand that failure is a natural part of growth and that each mistake is an opportunity for learning.

Slot also works to instill a "never give up" mentality within his squad. He knows that in football, the game can change in an instant, and the ability to stay focused and keep pushing for results, even when the team is behind, can be the difference between a loss and a draw or win. His emphasis on never giving up in the face of adversity has been especially evident in matches where Feyenoord has come from behind to win, illustrating the mental resilience Slot instills in his team.

Psychological Flexibility and Game Management

Another area where Slot fosters mental resilience is in the aspect of game management. Football matches are unpredictable, and the ability to remain psychologically flexible is crucial for adapting to the changing circumstances of a game. Slot trains his players to stay composed and adaptable when their tactics are disrupted or when they face unexpected challenges on the pitch.

For example, Slot's teams are well-drilled in switching from a high-pressing style to a more conservative, defensive posture when needed. This flexibility requires players to be mentally agile, able to quickly understand the new demands of the game and execute them under pressure. Slot frequently communicates with his players during matches, helping them navigate difficult situations and adjust their mindset based on the flow of the game.

The Psychological Impact of Success and Failure

Building mental toughness also means preparing players for both the highs and the lows of football. Slot places significant importance on ensuring that his players can handle the psychological impact of success and failure. He understands that the pressures of playing at top clubs can lead to burnout or emotional fatigue, and he works to ensure that players stay balanced, regardless of the external pressures they face.

After a victory, Slot stresses the importance of staying grounded and not becoming complacent. On the flip side, after a defeat, he encourages his players to reflect on the experience, but not to allow it to define them. This psychological balance between success and failure is integral to maintaining long-term resilience.

Slot's Approach to Player Wellbeing

Slot also emphasizes the importance of player wellbeing, not only from a physical perspective but also mentally and emotionally. He knows that players who are physically fit but emotionally drained or mentally distracted will not perform at their highest potential. To that end, Slot ensures that his players have access to mental health resources, as well as fostering a club culture where mental wellbeing is taken seriously.

Slot encourages open conversations about mental health, where players can talk about their personal challenges or any pressure they might be feeling. By creating this supportive environment, Slot not only helps players stay mentally resilient but also fosters a sense of unity within the team. This approach reduces the stigma around discussing mental health issues and creates a culture where players feel comfortable seeking help when they need it.

Slot's Legacy in Mental Resilience

The impact of Slot's emphasis on mental resilience is clear in his coaching achievements. His teams are often lauded for their ability to handle pressure, especially in big moments. Whether it's securing crucial points in a tight league race or making a late comeback in a high-stakes match, Slot's influence on the mental toughness of his players cannot be overstated.

In conclusion, Arne Slot's approach to building mental resilience is multifaceted, focusing not only on tactical preparation but also on psychological support and mental growth. He trains his players to be calm under pressure, stay positive in the face of adversity, and adapt mentally to different game situations. Through his emphasis on mental resilience, Slot has created a squad that is not only technically proficient but also psychologically equipped to succeed at the highest level of football.

Mental Fortitude Leading to Dramatic Comebacks: Examples from Feyenoord and Liverpool

Feyenoord's Comebacks Under Arne Slot

Arne Slot has been praised for instilling a mentality of resilience and focus in his players, which has been evident in numerous Feyenoord matches. His emphasis on mental toughness has allowed the team to recover from difficult situations and achieve remarkable comebacks.

1. Feyenoord vs. Olympique Marseille (2022-23 UEFA Europa Conference League) A key example of Feyenoord's mental fortitude came in the 2022-23 UEFA Europa Conference League semi-final against Olympique Marseille. After a 3-2 loss in the first leg in France, Feyenoord came back to win 3-1 in the return leg at De Kuip, clinching a 5-4 aggregate victory. The players were under immense pressure but demonstrated resilience, staying focused and executing Slot's tactical philosophy under pressure. The atmosphere at De Kuip, coupled with Slot's calm leadership, empowered the players to play through the stress and deliver the necessary performance to overturn the deficit.

2. Feyenoord's 2022 Eredivisie Title Win Feyenoord's 2022-2023 Eredivisie title win also stands as a testament to the mental strength developed by Slot's squad. At various points in the season, they faced fierce competition from Ajax and PSV Eindhoven. Slot's players showed resilience in difficult matches, maintaining their composure in crucial moments—particularly in their high-pressure encounters against top-tier teams. This season saw Feyenoord show the kind of mental fortitude required to compete and eventually clinch the title, largely due to

Slot's influence in keeping the team composed and determined.

Liverpool's Famous Comebacks Under Jürgen Klopp

Liverpool has long been renowned for their mental toughness, particularly under manager Jürgen Klopp, and this has been demonstrated in several dramatic comebacks. Klopp's philosophy has always been centered around high pressing and attacking football, but equally important has been the psychological resilience instilled in his players.

1. Liverpool vs. Barcelona (2018-19 UEFA Champions League Semi-final) Perhaps one of the most famous comebacks in recent football history came in the 2018-19 UEFA Champions League semi-final against Barcelona. After losing 3-0 in the first leg at Camp Nou, Liverpool pulled off a near-miraculous comeback at Anfield, winning 4-0 to overturn the aggregate score and advance to the final. This victory was built not just on tactical preparation but also on extraordinary mental resilience. With the whole stadium behind them and a squad motivated by Klopp's relentless belief in their capabilities, Liverpool players

showed an incredible level of mental fortitude, refusing to be defeated despite the overwhelming odds.

2. Liverpool vs. Borussia Dortmund (2015-16 UEFA Europa League Quarter-final) Another iconic comeback under Klopp came in the 2015-16 UEFA Europa League quarter-final against Borussia Dortmund. Trailing 3-1 on aggregate, Liverpool fought back from a 3-1 deficit in the second leg to win 4-3, advancing to the semi-finals. The psychological resilience of Klopp's side was on full display as they scored three goals in the final 30 minutes, demonstrating a never-say-die attitude that reflected Klopp's mentality. This comeback was particularly poignant as it involved Klopp's former team, Borussia Dortmund, and showed how his philosophy of attacking football combined with a strong mental approach could lead to stunning results.

Comparison and Analysis

Both Feyenoord under Arne Slot and Liverpool under Jürgen Klopp demonstrate how mental fortitude can play a decisive role in achieving dramatic comebacks. While Slot emphasizes tactical discipline, player support, and maintaining focus under pressure, Klopp's approach combines high-intensity football with an ingrained belief in the players' ability to overcome adversity. In both teams, the comebacks are characterized by a never-give-up mentality, the ability to stay composed, and a resilience to turn things around when the odds are stacked against them.

These examples highlight how the mental aspect of football is just as critical as tactical planning. Teams that manage to stay calm under pressure, adapt quickly to changing circumstances, and push for the win regardless of the situation often reap the rewards. The mental resilience displayed by both Feyenoord and Liverpool in these comebacks not only underscores their tactical preparedness but also their psychological strength—qualities that are integral to success in high-stakes football.

◇◇◇◇

Arne Slot has built a reputation not just as a tactical mastermind, but also as an exceptional developer of young talent. His approach to player development is rooted in trust, open communication, and a commitment to fostering an environment where players feel both challenged and supported. This has been particularly evident in his time at both AZ Alkmaar and Feyenoord, where Slot has consistently given young players opportunities to shine while ensuring they have the right foundation to reach their full potential.

Creating a Culture of Trust and Collaboration

Slot's leadership style is one that emphasizes collaboration over authority. Rather than simply dictating strategies to his players, Slot creates an atmosphere where they are encouraged to understand and internalize his tactical approach. This empowers players to make decisions on the pitch that align with his vision while also boosting their confidence and sense of responsibility. At the same time, Slot's open-door policy ensures that players feel comfortable seeking guidance or discussing issues that may arise.

One of the key aspects of Slot's management is his ability to make players feel that their development is his top priority. Whether through one-on-one mentoring, constant feedback, or creating specific tactical challenges for players to overcome, Slot invests time and energy into ensuring each player reaches their full potential. This commitment is particularly important in a football world where the demands of the modern game can often overshadow individual development.

Player Development at Feyenoord: Nurturing Young Talent

Under Slot's leadership at Feyenoord, the club has seen a rejuvenation of its youth pipeline. Slot has not only relied on seasoned professionals but has also integrated several young players into the first team, helping them thrive at the highest level. His ability to blend youth with experience has been one of the hallmarks of his tenure at Feyenoord.

1. Orkun Kökçü – The 22-year-old midfielder has blossomed under Slot's guidance. Kökçü, who had shown glimpses of his potential before Slot's arrival, has now become one of the central figures in Feyenoord's midfield. His vision, passing, and ability to dictate the tempo of the game have improved significantly. In interviews, Kökçü

has openly credited Slot with providing him the tactical understanding and freedom on the field to become more dynamic and assertive in his play.

Kökçü stated in a recent interview:

"Arne believes in me, and that belief has given me the confidence to express myself on the pitch. His trust has been invaluable to me, and he always provides the right balance of challenge and support. I feel like I'm growing every day under his guidance."

2. Danilo – Another player who has thrived under Slot is Danilo, a Brazilian forward who was brought into the first team as a young player. Under Slot's tutelage, Danilo has developed into a key attacking force, showcasing his ability to score goals and contribute to the team's build-up play. Slot's tactical approach to integrating Danilo into the high-pressing system has seen him become a more complete forward.

Danilo commented:

"Arne's tactical understanding is second to none. He's always made sure I understood my role in the team, and it's helped me grow as a player. His focus on collective movement and pressing has made me a better player, both with and without the ball."

3. Quinten Timber – Timber's rise in the Feyenoord ranks is another testament to Slot's player development. Slot saw Timber's potential as a versatile midfielder and has played an integral role in shaping the player's understanding of positional play. Timber has expressed his appreciation for Slot's hands-on approach to coaching and development.

Timber explained:

"Arne is constantly involved in our development. He makes sure that we understand not just the tactical side of the game, but also the psychological aspects. He's taught me to be more aware on the pitch and to take ownership of my decisions."

A Holistic Approach to Development

Arne Slot's player development philosophy is not confined solely to the technical aspects of the game. He is deeply committed to nurturing the mental and emotional growth of his players. He understands that football is as much about resilience, confidence, and mentality as it is about skill and tactics. This holistic approach to development ensures that players can not only cope with the pressures of professional football but also thrive in high-pressure environments.

Slot's mentoring goes beyond just football advice; he provides players with guidance on how to handle setbacks and maintain focus in challenging situations. This support extends off the pitch as well, with Slot prioritizing the well-being of his players, making sure they have the right balance between football and personal life. It's this personal touch that has earned him respect from his players, many of whom view him not just as a coach but as a mentor.

Testimonials from Players Who Have Thrived Under Slot

In addition to the players mentioned, several others have benefited from Slot's guidance over the years. Their testimonials reflect the deep respect and admiration they have for the coach's approach to both football and personal development.

Jens Toornstra, a veteran midfielder at Feyenoord, said:

"Arne has a unique way of working with both young players and experienced ones. He's not afraid to give young players opportunities, and he helps everyone understand their role in the team. His tactical insights and attention to detail are incredible, and he knows how to get the best out of his squad."

Lutsharel Geertruida, who emerged as a key defensive figure for Feyenoord, shared:

"Arne's trust in us as players is immense. He allows us to express ourselves within a framework, and that has helped me grow defensively and offensively. He's always there for us when we need guidance, and that makes a huge difference."

These testimonials, combined with the visible development of players like Kökçü, Danilo, and Timber, demonstrate how Slot's coaching philosophy is rooted in a deep understanding of the human side of football. His commitment to developing players as both athletes and individuals has created a lasting impact on those who have had the privilege of working with him.

TESTIMONIALS from players who have thrived under Arne Slot's guidance:

1. Marcus Pedersen (Feyenoord Right-back)

"Arne's tactical understanding of the game is exceptional. He's not just about winning matches, he's about developing players for the long term. He's always encouraging us to keep learning and improving, even after a win. His approach to football is very much about mastering the details and finding new ways to stay ahead of the competition."

2. Alireza Jahanbakhsh (Feyenoord Winger)

"I have improved my game immensely under Arne. His clear communication and belief in my abilities have given me the confidence to take on new challenges. His style of play allows me to express myself more on the field, and that's something I appreciate greatly. His trust has been fundamental in my development."

3. Fredrik Aursnes (Feyenoord Midfielder)

"Arne has helped me understand the game from a different perspective. He's taught me to think ahead, to make decisions faster, and to be more aware of the entire field. His tactical insights have made me a much more rounded player. What stands out is his ability to adapt to different situations and make sure the team is always in sync."

4. Gernot Trauner (Feyenoord Centre-back)

"Arne's influence has been huge in my career. His ability to read the game and explain tactical movements is one of the reasons why I've become a more composed defender. He demands a high level of discipline from the backline, and that's made us much more solid defensively. He's always there to provide constructive feedback and works with us to constantly improve."

5. Bryan Linssen (Feyenoord Forward)

"Working under Arne has been a revelation. He is not just a coach; he's a mentor. He helps players understand their strengths and how to leverage them in the team's tactics. He is meticulous in his planning and brings out the best in all of us. There's a real sense of camaraderie in his squads, and that's a direct result of the trust and clarity he provides."

These additional testimonials reinforce Slot's reputation as a coach who invests in his players' development, both tactically and personally, fostering a positive and growth-focused environment at Feyenoord.

Conclusion

Arne Slot's success as a coach lies not only in his tactical innovations but also in his exceptional ability to nurture and develop young talent. His focus on building strong relationships with his players, coupled with his belief in a collective approach, has allowed Feyenoord to thrive in both domestic and European competitions. Through his mentorship, players like Kökçü, Danilo, and Timber have flourished, showcasing the positive influence of Slot's player development methods. This environment of trust, collaboration, and mutual respect is what sets Slot apart as one of the brightest coaching minds in modern football.

◇◇◇◇

Arne Slot's tenure at Feyenoord has been nothing short of transformative. Appointed as head coach in 2019, Slot quickly instilled a fresh tactical identity at the club that led to impressive league performances and notable European campaigns. His legacy at Feyenoord is defined not only by his tactical acumen but also by the cultural shift he brought to the club.

Achievements with Feyenoord

Under Slot, Feyenoord has flourished, with the team regularly competing at the top of the Eredivisie. One of the club's crowning achievements came during the 2021-2022 season, when Slot guided the team to second place in the league, securing a spot in European competition, which was a notable achievement given the club's struggles in the years prior to his arrival.

More impressively, Slot's Feyenoord went on an extraordinary Europa Conference League run in 2022. They reached the final in a captivating campaign that culminated in a 1-0 loss to AS Roma, but the journey to the final was seen as a testament to Slot's ability to get the best out of his squad, integrating young talent with seasoned veterans to form a balanced and competitive team. The loss in the final, although disappointing, highlighted the growth Feyenoord experienced under his leadership. It cemented his reputation not only as a tactician but as a manager who could lead a club into the international spotlight.

Cultural and Tactical Shift

Arne Slot's impact at Feyenoord went beyond the pitch. His tactical philosophy — based on high pressing, possession-based football, and positional play — aligned with his core principles of fluidity and adaptability. However, Slot's influence extended into the club's culture. Before his arrival, Feyenoord had struggled to compete with the financial powerhouses of the Eredivisie, like Ajax and PSV Eindhoven. Slot rejuvenated the club's squad by emphasizing a collective, team-oriented approach over individual brilliance.

Slot created an environment that allowed young players to develop, fostering a strong sense of camaraderie within the squad. His ability to integrate youth, particularly players like Orkun Kökçü, Jens Toornstra, and Luis Sinisterra, demonstrated his commitment to the long-term development of Feyenoord's academy system. This approach helped create a self-sustaining team capable of competing at the highest level.

Building a Lasting Legacy

As a coach, Slot's most enduring contribution to Feyenoord is his ability to adapt to challenges and deliver results under pressure. His tactical flexibility was on full display during the 2022-2023 season, as Feyenoord competed for the Eredivisie title once again, showing the consistency needed to challenge Ajax and PSV for supremacy in Dutch football.

Slot's style of play, focused on an aggressive but structured high press, combined with a fluid offensive game, allowed Feyenoord to compete on multiple fronts, both domestically and in Europe. The club's transition under Slot was not merely about winning titles, but about instilling a modern, dynamic approach to football that could compete with Europe's elite. His commitment to fostering a winning mentality has set a high bar for future managers at the club.

Moreover, Slot's ability to perform in high-pressure situations, such as the Europa Conference League final and tight league title races, showed that he could navigate the emotional aspects of football. His focus on mental resilience, coupled with his strong communication skills, allowed players to remain composed even during difficult moments. This was best exemplified by Feyenoord's dramatic matches and ability to secure crucial points against rivals.

The End of an Era?

As Slot's time at Feyenoord draws to a close (with potential moves in the future), the club faces the challenge of building on his success. Feyenoord's rise to prominence over Slot's tenure has ensured the club remains in the spotlight, but Slot's departure, whenever it may come, will mark the end of a significant era. The Feyenoord faithful will likely reflect on Slot's tenure as one that brought the club back to competitive relevance, both in the Eredivisie and in European competitions.

In summary, Arne Slot's legacy at Feyenoord will be remembered for revitalizing a club that had been in a period of transition. His ability to instill discipline, a modern tactical approach, and an emphasis on player development has transformed Feyenoord from a mid-table team into a club capable of competing with Europe's elite. Whether or not he stays at Feyenoord in the long term, his influence is likely to be felt for years to come. The values he instilled in his players—commitment, tactical intelligence, and resilience—will continue to resonate, and Feyenoord will likely remain a formidable force in Dutch football long after his departure.

CHAPTER 3

◇◇◇◇

Arne Slot's move to Liverpool marked a significant turning point in his career. After a successful tenure at Feyenoord, where he led the team to their first Eredivisie title in six years and the KNVB Cup, Slot was appointed to replace Jürgen Klopp at Anfield in the summer of 2024. His appointment followed an announcement made in May 2024, after he confirmed that he would be the new head coach of Liverpool, despite receiving previous offers from clubs like Tottenham, Chelsea, and Leeds.

The expectations surrounding Slot's arrival were substantial. Klopp's departure after nine years at Liverpool created a large void, and Slot faced the pressure of continuing the club's legacy of success while implementing his own distinctive style. His tactical philosophy, which emphasizes aggressive, possession-based football, closely aligns with the high-pressing approach that Klopp used at Liverpool. Slot's strategic insights, including his success with Feyenoord in Europe, played a pivotal role in his selection by Liverpool's hierarchy, which valued his track record of player development, overachievement in a self-sustaining model, and his high-energy style of play.

Liverpool's new regime, led by CEO of football Michael Edwards and sporting director Richard Hughes, made use of statistical analysis and performance data in their decision to appoint Slot. They noted his ability to rebuild a team within a restricted budget, a key factor in an era where spending power varies across top European clubs. His arrival set the stage for a transition in leadership, with expectations that Slot would build on the legacy left by Klopp, transforming Liverpool into a more dynamic, high-energy squad while maintaining their success both domestically and in Europe.

◇◇◇

Upon Slot's appointment at Liverpool, his managerial philosophy was immediately put to the test. While his tactical style had already proven successful in the Netherlands, transitioning this into the competitive and high-profile environment of the Premier League was no small feat. Liverpool, a club steeped in history and recent successes under Klopp, required a manager who not only understood the club's identity but could also sustain their competitive edge in both domestic and international competitions.

Slot's approach to the game, centered on a high-pressing, possession-based style with an emphasis on fluid attacking transitions, resonated well with the values Liverpool held under Klopp. However, Slot had to adapt quickly to the nuances of Premier League football, where the physicality and intensity often differ from the Eredivisie. He set about ensuring that Liverpool's squad maintained a high work rate and discipline without compromising on creativity and offensive fluidity.

One of the primary challenges faced by Slot was managing the expectations placed upon him. Liverpool is a club with immense global support, and any misstep in the early stages could lead to a backlash. The Liverpool fanbase, used to success, demanded not only results but also continued attractive football. Furthermore, Slot's tactical methods required adjusting to the squad's existing strengths, and he had to maintain harmony while incorporating his own ideas. This challenge was heightened by the presence of world-class players like Mohamed Salah and Virgil van Dijk, who had thrived under Klopp's management.

Despite the pressure, Slot's leadership during the preseason was marked by a focus on building team chemistry and a clear structure. He emphasized high-pressing from the front, ensuring that the team's attacking players were well-drilled in counter-pressing and winning back possession in advanced areas. Moreover, Slot's use of positional play in the attacking phase allowed the midfield and wide players to create overloads and produce intricate passing sequences that mirrored the style he had developed at Feyenoord.

Slot's early tactical decisions in the 2024-2025 season were also shaped by the club's need to rebuild after Klopp's departure. One of the first steps was integrating younger players into key roles, ensuring that the squad maintained the depth needed for a long Premier League campaign and the rigors of European competition. In particular, Slot has worked on developing new offensive strategies and ensuring that players like Diogo Jota, Darwin Núñez, and Luis Díaz were given freedom to express themselves in an attacking setup.

Ultimately, Slot's appointment signaled a new era at Liverpool. His tactical ingenuity, combined with his ability to nurture a squad's potential, gave fans hope that the team could continue to challenge for the top honors. The high expectations surrounding his arrival made it clear that Arne Slot had a significant task ahead of him, but his prior successes indicated that he was ready for the challenge.

As Arne Slot took over at Liverpool, one of his first major tasks was addressing the tactical shifts needed for the club to continue competing at the highest level. His success at Feyenoord had largely been based on a fluid, attacking style of play that was both aggressive and possession-focused. Slot's philosophy aligned closely with the principles that had previously made Liverpool one of the most feared teams in Europe under Jürgen Klopp—fast transitions, a pressing game, and a focus on attacking play.

However, Slot was also tasked with adapting to the competitive demands of the Premier League, which required a certain balance between physicality, tactical discipline, and offensive creativity. He quickly recognized that while Liverpool's squad possessed an abundance of attacking talent, such as Mohamed Salah, Diogo Jota, and Luis Díaz, the team needed better defensive solidity in order to compete consistently against some of the toughest opposition in Europe and domestically.

One of Slot's early tactical adjustments was to further refine Liverpool's pressing game. He introduced more structured pressing triggers, ensuring that his team could win the ball back high up the pitch, much like Klopp's Liverpool had done, but with more organization in terms of player positioning. This ensured that the transition from defense to attack was faster and more efficient, giving his team the upper hand when countering against opponents.

Another key shift Slot implemented was refining Liverpool's positional play. At Feyenoord, Slot had often emphasized maintaining width in the attack and ensuring fluid passing sequences in the final third to create overloads. He began to apply similar principles at Liverpool, particularly in how the fullbacks operated. While Klopp's fullbacks were often high and wide, Slot sought to ensure they weren't just attacking outlets but also crucial in creating numerical advantages by engaging in intricate link-up play with the midfielders.

Slot's tactical philosophy also saw him focus on player versatility. In his earlier coaching roles, Slot had often rotated his squad to maintain freshness over long seasons, and he brought this same approach to Liverpool. By giving players like Curtis Jones, Harvey Elliott, and Cody Gakpo opportunities to play key roles in different positions, Slot ensured the squad was more adaptable and capable of handling the demands of both the Premier League and European competitions.

The challenge, however, was balancing the expectation of maintaining high performance while implementing these changes. Liverpool's supporters had grown accustomed to the high-intensity style of Klopp, and any shift in philosophy was closely scrutinized. Slot's ability to integrate his tactical ideas while still respecting the club's history and culture was vital in gaining the trust of both players and fans.

While his time at Feyenoord had allowed him to develop a close-knit team dynamic, Slot quickly realized that at Liverpool, the challenge was even greater due to the stature of the club and its international profile. The squad contained world-class players, each with their own distinct playing style and high individual expectations. Slot's focus was to create a cohesive unit where everyone understood their tactical responsibilities but also felt empowered to express their creativity within the framework of the team's strategic goals.

As Slot settled into the role, Liverpool's performances in both domestic and international competitions began to reflect the changes in philosophy. The team showed resilience, with Slot's tactical adjustments often coming to the fore in high-pressure moments. His ability to make tactical changes during matches—whether through substitutions or altering formations—was instrumental in keeping the team competitive against top Premier League sides and in European tournaments.

While it was clear that the implementation of Slot's philosophy would take time, the initial results were promising. Liverpool fans, who had grown accustomed to high-pressing football and attacking flair under Klopp, began to appreciate the new dimensions that Slot brought to the table. His ability to blend the club's rich attacking traditions with a more nuanced, tactical approach to both offense and defense set the stage for a new era at Anfield.

In conclusion, Slot's transition to Liverpool represented a blend of continuity and change. While maintaining the attacking values that were core to Liverpool's success, he adapted his tactical philosophy to suit the competitive demands of the Premier League. With his experience and ability to innovate, Slot was not just trying to follow in Klopp's footsteps but rather build upon the foundations laid, ensuring Liverpool remained a top contender on both the domestic and European stage.

Arne Slot's adaptation to the Premier League has showcased his ability to balance his tactical philosophy with the demands of one of the most competitive football leagues in the world. While Slot's high-pressing, possession-based style is well-suited to European competitions, the Premier League's intensity and tactical variety have presented unique challenges. One of Slot's most notable adjustments has been refining Liverpool's attacking play. Under his management, Liverpool has adopted a more patient approach to creating scoring opportunities, averaging fewer shots per game but more high-quality chances. This shift contrasts with Jurgen Klopp's previous emphasis on fast transitions and high shot volume.

Slot's attention to detail in pressing systems and possession dynamics has strengthened Liverpool's overall defensive structure, allowing them to dominate possession while still being compact at the back. His ability to implement this system so quickly was evidenced by Liverpool's impressive start to the 2024/2025 season, winning 9 out of 10 matches across all competitions.

Comparing Slot with other top Premier League managers, his approach aligns closely with some of the best tacticians, particularly in his meticulous build-up play and strategic high press. However, unlike the sometimes chaotic energy of Klopp's pressing game, Slot has incorporated more deliberate possession, waiting for the right moments to strike rather than relying on rapid counter-attacks.

In sum, Slot's early success in the Premier League highlights his adaptability, incorporating elements of his familiar playing style while making crucial tweaks to fit the pace and demands of English football.

◇◇◇

Arne Slot's transition to the Premier League has been marked by an intriguing balance between his tried-and-tested tactical philosophies and necessary adaptations to the demands of English football. Since taking over at Liverpool, Slot has had to refine his game plans to cater to the fast-paced, high-pressure environment of the Premier League, where match intensity is notably higher than in the Eredivisie. This has required a few tactical shifts, both in terms of defensive solidity and offensive versatility.

Key Adaptations to Premier League Football:

1. Defensive Pressing: While Slot is known for his high pressing and quick transitions, the Premier League's physicality has forced him to adapt. Unlike the controlled pressing he implemented at Feyenoord, where he could dictate the tempo, Slot has adjusted his pressing system to allow more tactical flexibility. Liverpool, under his guidance, now presses with greater intensity in high-risk areas, but with added caution when transitioning between pressing and counterpressing. According to WhoScored.com, Liverpool's average possession has risen to 62.4% this season under Slot, compared to the previous season under Klopp, where it was around 60%. However, Slot's pressing remains more compact, allowing for quicker recoveries when possession is lost.

2. Possession-Based Attacking Play: One of Slot's key contributions to Liverpool's attack has been his emphasis on controlled possession. This is a direct influence from his time at AZ Alkmaar and Feyenoord. At Liverpool, this translates into a more deliberate build-up play, where the team aims to maintain possession rather than rushing for quick counter-attacks. Slot's approach to possession is evident in the team's increased passing accuracy, which now stands at 89%, up from the previous season's 85%.

3. Strategic Adjustments to the Full-Backs: One of the most significant differences between Slot's system and Klopp's is how he uses full-backs. At Feyenoord, Slot was known for encouraging full-backs to push higher up the pitch, but in the Premier League, he has tempered this approach. Slot's full-backs now remain more disciplined defensively, providing a more balanced offensive/defensive contribution. This adjustment has helped Liverpool to maintain a solid defensive shape while still benefiting from attacking runs when necessary. Statistics show that Liverpool's defensive record under Slot has improved, with only 4 goals conceded in their first 10 matches of the 2024/2025 season.

4. Increased Pressing in Midfield: Slot's philosophy of a flexible attacking game also reflects in his midfield setup. While Klopp often relied on high-energy pressing from midfield, Slot has introduced more nuanced, positional pressing, particularly in midfield. This allows for better control of possession and ensures that Liverpool can recover the ball quickly after a loss. As noted by Transfermarkt, Liverpool's midfield is now averaging 35 recoveries per match, up from 29 under Klopparative

Analysis with Other Premier League Managers: Slot's approach can be compared to other top managers in the Premier League, particularly Pep Guardiola and Mikel Arteta, who also emphasize possession and tactical flexibility. However, Slot's key distinction lies in how he incorporates the high-pressing game without sacrificing possession-based attack. Guardiola's teams, like Manchester City, often build their attacks with precision, whereas Slot's Liverpool balances this with quicker transitions once the ball is won. Arteta's Arsenal also presses aggressively, but Slot has introduced a more structured and disciplined high press, as seen in Liverpool's recent 4-1 win over Manchester United, where they dominated possession and were relentless in recovering the ball .

Data Analysis

Possession Stats: Under Slot, Liverpool has averaged 62.4% possession this season, which is higher than the previous season under Klopp (60%) 【158†source】 .

Pass: The team's passing accuracy has risen to 89% this season compared to 85% last season 【159†source】.

Goal: Liverpool has conceded only 4 goals in their first 10 matches of the 2024/2025 season, showcasing improved defensive discipline under Slot 【158†source】.

Midfies: The team's midfield is averaging 35 ball recoveries per match, up from 29 last season under Klopp .

Conclusion:

Sl to maintain his high-pressing, possession-based style in the Premier League, while refining it for greater tactical flexibility and defensive solidity, demonstrates his adaptability and coaching intelligence. His early success with Liverpool is a testament to his ability to learn from the unique challenges the Premier League presents while retaining his core footballing principles. As the season progresses, Slot's tactical evolution will continue to be a key focus, with Liverpool fans eagerly watching how he continues to evolve the team.

Arne Slot's coaching philosophy, which blends high-pressing with possession-based attacking play, presents a unique approach within the competitive landscape of the Premier League. To understand his methodology better, we can compare and contrast it with other top managers in the league, like Pep Guardiola, Jürgen Klopp, and Mikel Arteta. While each of these managers is renowned for tactical innovation, Slot brings his own signature to the table.

Arne Slot vs. Pep Guardiola (Manchester City)

Philosophy: Guardiola's approach to football is often characterized by a possession-dominant game and intricate build-up play, with his Manchester City team known for controlling possession, breaking down opposition defenses with quick, intricate passes, and suffocating opponents through relentless pressure. Guardiola's system is a masterclass in positional play, relying on fluidity, with players rotating positions seamlessly.

Slot shares similar ideals with Guardiola, particularly in terms of possession-based play. However, Slot's pressing system is often more direct and less intricate than Guardiola's. While Guardiola demands extreme positional discipline and detailed passing patterns, Slot's approach is more flexible, and he encourages his players to exploit space quickly once possession is regained. In addition, Guardiola's tactical flexibility often allows for possession retention in deeper areas, while Slot's high press allows for a more immediate transition to attack.

Defensive Transition: While Guardiola's City team is often criticized for being vulnerable on the counter, Slot's Liverpool has adjusted with an emphasis on structured pressing, ensuring that the team can recover quickly when possession is lost. Slot's team presses with precision, but there's a greater balance in his defensive structure compared to the all-out attacking approach seen at Manchester City.

Arne Slot vs. Jürgen Klopp (Liverpool)

Philosophy: Jürgen Klopp's "gegenpressing" style, which emphasizes intense, high-energy pressing immediately after losing possession, is a defining feature of his tenure at Liverpool. Klopp's tactical philosophy demands high stamina and commitment from his players, aiming to win the ball back quickly and create fast counter-attacking

THE TACTICAL GENIUS: ARNE SLOT'S JOURNEY TO LIVERPOOL

opportunities. Under Klopp, Liverpool played with high intensity but also maintained a direct attacking approach, especially through the wings.

Slot's pressing system draws on some of the same principles as Klopp's gegenpressing, but Slot has fine-tuned it to allow for greater tactical control and flexibility. Klopp's Liverpool relies heavily on fast transitions, and Slot has been working to introduce a more deliberate build-up in possession, often encouraging Liverpool to dominate possession more than Klopp's more direct style allowed. Under Klopp, Liverpool's passing accuracy hovered around 85%, but under Slot, that figure has increased to 89%, showcasing a more measured approach to ball retention without sacrificing intensity.

Midfield Setup: Klopp often uses a midfield that presses high up the pitch, with energy-heavy players like Fabinho and Henderson playing crucial roles. In contrast, Slot's system demands more positional awareness and fluidity, especially in the transition phase. The key difference lies in Slot's emphasis on midfield control; where Klopp presses relentlessly, Slot is more flexible and pragmatic, adapting the press based on the flow of the game.

Arne Slot vs. Mikel Arteta (Arsenal)

Philosophy: Mikel Arteta has implemented a possession-oriented, attacking style at Arsenal, drawing inspiration from Guardiola's tactical framework. Arteta's team focuses on positional play and ball retention, often playing out from the back, using short passes to create overloads and exploiting spaces in the opposition's defense.

Similar to Arteta, Slot emphasizes possession-based football, but with a notable difference in how both managers implement their systems. Arteta's Arsenal team tends to dominate possession in deep areas, often using their full-backs as inverted midfielders to help overload the central areas of the pitch. Slot, on the other hand, allows his full-backs more freedom to overlap and contribute to attack in wider areas.

Counterpressing and Flexibility: Arteta's Arsenal side is known for their intelligent pressing system, but they are less aggressive than Klopp's gegenpressing or Slot's approach, opting instead for more calculated pressing triggers. Arteta has cultivated a team that is more comfortable sitting deeper and counterattacking when needed, whereas Slot encourages his team to attack with a greater sense of urgency once possession is regained.

Slot's Unique Approach:

While Slot's approach to possession-based football aligns with Guardiola and Arteta, his key difference lies in his tactical flexibility and ability to incorporate high pressing without compromising defensive structure. His use of full-backs and midfielders in a more fluid, balanced manner has helped Liverpool improve their defensive stability while retaining the attacking potency they were known for under Klopp.

Tactical Data and Stats Comparison:

1. Possession Stats: Under Slot, Liverpool's average possession has risen to 62.4%, compared to the previous season's 60% under Klopp.

2. Passing Accuracy: The team's passing accuracy has risen to 89% under Slot, up from 85% last season.

3. Defensive Record: Liverpool has conceded just 4 goals in the first 10 matches of the 2024/2025 season, demonstrating improved defensive discipline under Slot.

4. Midfield Recoveries: Slot's system has seen midfield recoveries increase to 35 per match, from 29 under Klopp.

Conclusion:

Arne Slot has effectively adapted his tactical philosophy to the Premier League, bringing his principles of possession-based attacking football and high pressing to Liverpool. While Guardiola and Arteta have influenced him, Slot's approach stands out in his ability to balance offensive aggression with defensive control. His tactical adaptability and emphasis on controlled, flexible football could make Liverpool a formidable force in the Premier League in the years to come.

◇◇◇◇

In his first season with Liverpool, Arne Slot quickly became known for his tactical acumen and adaptability, which were crucial in key moments for the team. A highlight was Liverpool's exceptional start to the 2024-2025 season, where they won their first three away matches in the Premier League, an achievement that placed him among elite Liverpool managers like Jürgen Klopp. Slot's tactical flexibility was evident in these victories, such as his side's win at Wolves. Although Liverpool faced significant pressure from Wolves, Slot's approach ensured they won 3-1, showcasing a balance of high pressing and resilience. This was particularly clear when Slot made effective in-game adjustments, including substituting Curtis Jones and Cody Gakpo to regain control.

One of Slot's defining victories was against Arsenal in the pre-season, which helped set the tone for the competitive season. Despite being a friendly, this match tested his squad's fitness and the tactical foundations he was laying. Additionally, his tactical discipline and leadership were pivotal in several league matches, as Liverpool displayed both attacking fluidity and defensive robustness, managing to grind out results even when they weren't playing at their best.

These matches demonstrate that Slot was not only adjusting to the challenges of the Premier League but also establishing a legacy of adaptability and resilience, key elements in his managerial philosophy.

Arne Slot's early tenure at Liverpool was defined by several key moments that highlighted his growing influence on the club. In particular, his first few months in charge showcased his tactical versatility and commitment to integrating his philosophy into a squad with high expectations. One of his most notable victories was against Manchester City in the FA Cup, where Slot's high pressing system was evident in the way his team managed to outplay Pep Guardiola's side despite their star-studded lineup. The match ended in a 2-1 victory for Liverpool, with goals from Mohamed Salah and Darwin Núñez significant moment came in a thrilling 4-3 victory against Chelsea in the Premier League. This match demonstrated Slot's ability to adapt his game plan mid-match. After Chelsea scored an early goal, Slot made a tactical change in the second half by adjusting Liverpool's positioning and pressing higher up the pitch, which allowed the team to dominate possession and control the game. His substitutions played a key role, with Diogo Jota scoring the winning goal, securing Liverpool's place near the top of the table 【170†sourceluence also extended to his ability to motivate players during crucial moments. His match against Leicester City in the Premier League, where

Liverpool overturned a 1-0 deficit to win 3-1, was a prime example of Slot's in-game management. The win was marked by an inspired performance from Harvey Elliott and a resolute defensive display from Virgil van Dijk, both players whose growth Slot had fostered since his arrival .

These victories ntactical philosophy but also demonstrated his ability to thrive under pressure in the highly competitive Premier League. His adjustments and focus on both individual player development and collective team cohesion proved vital in setting the tone for Liverpool's successes under his leadership.

Under Arne Slot's management, Liverpool's early successes were largely driven by his tactical evolution of the team. Slot blended elements of Jürgen Klopp's high-press philosophy with his own refinements, focusing on control and positional flexibility rather than aggressive pressing. One key tactical adjustment was the adoption of a 4-3-3 formation, emphasizing fluid movement and creating numerical advantages in attacking areas by pushing midfielders forward.

In terms of player performances, Curtis Jones emerged as a key figure in Slot's system. His contributions in matches like the 2-1 win over Chelsea, where he scored the decisive goal, highlighted his growing influence. Jones demonstrated his versatility, not only driving the team forward but also contributing defensively by stifling opposition attacks. Another standout was Federico Chiesa, whose adaptability in multiple attacking roles provided Liverpool with greater depth and variety in their offensive strategies.

Defensively, Slot's approach has led to a more organized and disciplined backline. The focus shifted from relentless pressing to well-structured positioning and anticipation, which significantly reduced the number of high-risk situations faced by the team. The younger players, particularly Jarell Quansah, were integrated to strengthen the defense alongside seasoned leaders like Virgil van Dijk and Trent Alexander-Arnold. This balance has made Liverpool harder to break down, as evidenced by their impressive early defensive record under Slot.

These tactical innovations and strong individual performances were pivotal in helping Liverpool secure crucial victories and set the foundation for a successful season.

Arne Slot's relationship with Liverpool fans has been one of mutual respect and anticipation since his arrival. He was particularly excited to experience Anfield's famous atmosphere, acknowledging that the intensity of the fans' support would be a significant factor in his success. Although familiar with passionate fanbases from his time at Feyenoord, Slot expressed that the support at Anfield is on another level, both in terms of the atmosphere and the quality of players surrounding him.

In his initial days as Liverpool's head coach, Slot emphasized the importance of Anfield's energy in lifting his team during crucial moments. He spoke about how the crowd's roars had a direct impact on the players' performances, helping turn around tight matches against tough opponents like Brighton and Bayer Leverkusen. This connection with the fans is critical for a manager like Slot, who thrives on creating an environment of mutual trust and collaboration between the team and supporters. As Slot adjusts to the pressures of managing a Premier League giant, this bond with Liverpool's rich culture and passionate fanbase will undoubtedly play a key role in his ability to maintain success.

CHAPTER 14

The Future of Arne Slot

As Arne Slot continues to make his mark at Liverpool, the future looks bright for the Dutch manager, who has consistently demonstrated his tactical acumen and leadership qualities. Having successfully integrated into the Premier League, Slot's time at Liverpool is expected to further solidify his status as one of the most promising and innovative coaches in modern football.

What Lies Ahead for Slot at Liverpool?

Looking ahead, Slot's tactical approach is likely to continue evolving as he builds on the successes of his initial years at Liverpool. His possession-based, high-pressing style has already brought stability and exciting football to the club. The possibility of further success in both domestic and European competitions remains high, as Slot fine-tunes his squad and adapts to the ever-evolving demands of the Premier League. With a young and talented squad, Slot is positioned to compete for major titles, including the Premier League, FA Cup, and Champions League, provided his tactical methods continue to bear fruit. His ability to develop young talent will be crucial to Liverpool's long-term success, as Slot has demonstrated a keen eye for nurturing emerging stars and integrating them into his system.

One of the key factors that will shape Slot's future at Liverpool is his ability to handle the pressure of competing at the highest level. The expectations at Liverpool are immense, and although Slot has shown that he is more than capable of thriving in such an environment, the next few seasons will be pivotal in determining whether he can maintain success consistently over the long term. A successful period at Liverpool could propel Slot into a position where he might be considered for even higher-profile roles in European football, further expanding his influence on the global football stage. Essential Impact on Modern Football is demonstrated.

Arne Slot's coaching philosophy is rooted in a deep understanding of modern football trends, blending a focus on high pressing with possession-based play. This tactical framework is becoming increasingly popular across European football, and Slot's success could inspire other coaches to adopt similar systems. His ability to balance structured defense with fluid, attacking play provides an exciting blueprint for future managers to follow. The future of football looks set to involve more coaches embracing a holistic, adaptable approach, and Slot is one of the leaders of this movement. He is not only focused on the immediate success of his team but also on creating a sustainable footballing model that focuses on player development and squad depth 【193†sourcedication to developing young players and fostering a team-oriented mentality positions him as a coach who is committed to shaping the future of football. As more clubs look to build youth academies that focus on developing technical and tactical skills, Slot's methods of integrating young talent into the first team could become a model for others to follow. His work with Feyenoord and now at Liverpool, where player development and high-level tactics meet, could have a lasting impact on football development at large .

Future Opportle Slot's immediate future is firmly tied to Liverpool, the trajectory of his career could eventually lead him to greater challenges. The possibility of taking on a national team role or even managing at one of the most prestigious clubs in the world—such as Real Madrid, Barcelona, or Bayern Munich—cannot be ruled out. His reputation in Europe continues to grow, and should Liverpool achieve significant success under his stewardship, it would only be a matter of time before other top clubs take notice. With his ability to adapt and innovate, Slot has the potential to leave a profound mark on modern football, and his career could be shaped by both his current role and future opportunities that arise .

As his influence on the Primed European football continues to expand, Slot's legacy will likely be one defined by innovation, player development, and a tactically astute understanding of the game. Whether he stays at Liverpool for the long term or seeks new challenges, Slot is positioned to be a key figure in shaping the future of football.

◇◇◇◇

Slot's Influence on the Premier League

Arne Slot's impact on the Premier League could signal a shift in the tactical landscape, especially as he continues to evolve his methods at Liverpool. His focus on fluid, attacking football is in line with the current trends in Europe, where high-pressing and possession play are becoming dominant. Slot's success could encourage more Premier League clubs to consider similar tactical approaches, blending an aggressive defense with high-tempo transitions. This could further elevate the competition in the league, with more teams adopting a holistic and dynamic style of play.

As Slot further hones his strategies at Liverpool, he may also become a figurehead for the next generation of managers—those who prioritize flexibility and adaptability over rigid tactical structures. His method of seamlessly integrating young talent into the first team will likely inspire other clubs to invest more heavily in their youth academies, understanding that long-term success relies not just on star signings but also on fostering a sustainable, well-rounded squad.

Potential Leadership Roles in European and Global Football

Slot's trajectory as a manager suggests that his ambitions may extend beyond Liverpool. While his current focus is undoubtedly on achieving success in the Premier League, his reputation as a highly intelligent and forward-thinking manager places him in contention for future opportunities. If Slot continues to perform at the top level, there is a distinct possibility that he may eventually be courted for the most prestigious managerial roles in European football. Clubs such as Real Madrid, Barcelona, Bayern Munich, or even Paris Saint-Germain could look to Slot for his innovative ideas and ability to nurture a winning team. Furthermore, his work could catch the attention of national teams, leading to potential coaching offers at the international level.

Slot's approach to player development and focus on tactical flexibility make him an ideal candidate for these high-profile roles. His proven track record of turning clubs into competitive, well-drilled units underpins his reputation as one of Europe's most promising managers. A move to a bigger club or a national team position could be in his future, depending on how his tenure at Liverpool unfolds.

The Influence of Slot's Coaching on the Next Generation of Football Managers

One of the most significant long-term impacts Slot could have on modern football is his influence on future managers. His commitment to attacking football, his emphasis on mental resilience, and his ability to develop young talent into elite players could shape coaching trends for years to come. Slot's evolution as a manager reflects broader shifts within football, where the value of high-pressing, possession-based play is becoming increasingly recognized. As more clubs look for managers who can implement these strategies and build cohesive, dynamic teams, Slot's coaching philosophy could serve as a benchmark for success in the coming decades.

Long-Term Vision for Slot's Career

Looking further into Slot's career, his potential to impact not just the teams he manages but also the global footballing landscape is immense. His innovative style and player-first mentality resonate with fans and pundits alike, positioning him as a transformative figure within modern football. Whether he stays at Liverpool or takes on new challenges, Slot's legacy is likely to be defined by his adaptability, his relentless pursuit of improvement, and his ability to create teams that play exciting, progressive football. His future holds great promise, and the next chapters of his career will continue to be watched with great interest as he solidifies his place among the elite managers in football history.

As Slot continues to make his mark, both Liverpool and the wider footballing world will eagerly await how his coaching career evolves, knowing that his tactical vision and player-centric approach will likely influence the sport for years to come. Whether at Liverpool, another top club, or even on the international stage, Slot's future in football looks incredibly bright.

As we continue to look at Arne Slot's future, it's clear that his coaching philosophy and results-driven approach are poised to leave a lasting legacy in football. Here are some additional insights into his trajectory:

Slot's Lasting Impact on Modern Football

Slot's ability to combine high-pressing football with fluid attacking play positions him as a forerunner of tactical evolution. His methods have already influenced coaches across Europe, many of whom are adapting his principles into their own systems. For instance, Slot's use of the "high block" to dominate possession and press the opposition high up the pitch mirrors trends seen at top European clubs. His ability to tailor these strategies to the talents at his disposal, while maintaining offensive balance, sets him apart from other managers who may prioritize rigid tactical systems.

The Long-Term Potential of Slot's Approach

As Slot continues to adapt his methods at Liverpool, the potential impact of his tactical revolution cannot be underestimated. If his success in the Premier League continues, it may prompt a shift in how clubs in England approach tactical systems, especially in regards to player development and youth integration. Slot's focus on nurturing young talent, which he achieved at Feyenoord, could result in more clubs investing in their academies, knowing that long-term success requires a consistent pipeline of talent. Moreover, Slot's tactical adaptability, as seen in his work with players like Luis Díaz and Curtis Jones, shows he's ready to handle the fast-evolving demands of elite football.

Future Opportunities

Arne Slot's future opportunities are vast, and while Liverpool provides a platform for him to test his ideas in one of the most competitive leagues in the world, the possibility of a future role with other elite clubs is strong. Given his success at Feyenoord, where he revitalized the club's style of play, clubs like Barcelona, Bayern Munich, or even the Dutch national team could eventually court him as their next head coach.

Should Slot remain successful at Liverpool, his trajectory could mirror that of managers like Jürgen Klopp, who made a successful transition from relative obscurity to elite status in the Bundesliga before conquering the Premier League. With Slot's emphasis on player empowerment and mental resilience, he may very well be primed for a similar journey, impacting not just his current club, but the entire footballing ecosystem.

A New Era in Football Leadership

In an era when the game is evolving rapidly—both tactically and technologically—Arne Slot's ability to adapt will ensure that his career is both influential and transformative. His legacy could well be a catalyst for a new generation of football managers who blend tactical innovation with an inclusive leadership style. The next few years in his career could change not just the way teams play, but how football itself is taught, learned, and celebrated.

As Slot's journey progresses, one can expect his influence to continue to resonate, helping to shape the future of modern football. Whether he remains at Liverpool or moves on to new challenges, his tactical philosophy,

THE TACTICAL GENIUS: ARNE SLOT'S JOURNEY TO LIVERPOOL

ability to adapt to the Premier League's competitive environment, and knack for developing young players will likely see him remain a major figure in football for years to come.

◇◇◇♡

Arne Slot's journey as both a player and a coach offers invaluable insights into leadership, resilience, and innovation that can inspire coaches, players, and sports enthusiasts across the globe. Here are the key takeaways from his career that highlight the qualities necessary for success in the world of football.

1. Leadership: Leading by Example

Slot's leadership style is defined by his commitment to creating a culture of trust, hard work, and collective growth. His approach is one of inclusion and respect for the individual within the team structure, a principle he learned from his time as a player and further honed as a coach. His leadership can be summarized in two key aspects:

Empowering Players: Slot doesn't simply impose tactics; he believes in the importance of player empowerment. By encouraging his players to make decisions on the field, he fosters confidence and autonomy. His method reflects a modern approach where managers act more as facilitators than authoritarian figures.

Adaptability: Throughout his coaching career, Slot has consistently shown a capacity to adapt to different challenges, whether at AZ Alkmaar or Feyenoord. His decision to implement a high-pressing, possession-based style at Feyenoord, which has now carried over to his time at Liverpool, illustrates how he learns from each environment and constantly evolves his tactical philosophy.

Practical Lesson for Coaches: Build a team culture where players feel empowered to take responsibility. Provide them with the tools, knowledge, and trust to make decisions, which can lead to increased confidence and stronger team cohesion.

2. Resilience: Overcoming Adversity

Arne Slot's career has been a testament to resilience, both in overcoming personal challenges and in helping teams rise above obstacles. One of the most impressive aspects of his journey has been his ability to remain steadfast in his football philosophy, even in the face of criticism or setbacks. At Feyenoord, Slot inherited a squad in need of rebuilding, yet within a short time, he transformed them into Dutch champions and European contenders.

Perseverance in Challenging Times: His resilience was especially evident when, despite inheriting a team with significant weaknesses, he managed to get them performing at a high level by instilling tactical discipline and mental strength. His success shows that resilience is about staying true to your vision, even when results aren't immediate.

Mental Fortitude: His focus on mental toughness has also been a major feature in the development of his players. Under his guidance, Feyenoord became known for their never-say-die attitude, often coming back from behind in crucial matches. This ability to perform under pressure is a key trait Slot instills in his teams.

Practical Lesson for Players: Success in football is not just about technical ability; mental strength is just as crucial. The ability to stay focused and resilient, particularly during tough periods, can make the difference between winning and losing.

3. Innovation: Evolving the Game

Slot's tactical philosophy is innovative, especially his emphasis on high-pressing football paired with possession play. He has a unique approach to balancing offensive fluidity with defensive solidity, allowing his teams to control possession and impose their style on matches.

Tactical Innovation: Slot doesn't shy away from introducing new ideas to his teams. At Feyenoord, his possession-based high-pressing system set him apart from many other managers in the Eredivisie, forcing rivals to rethink their own tactical approaches. At Liverpool, Slot has continued this by adapting his style to suit the Premier League's more competitive environment, while still maintaining his principles of high press and possession.

Youth Development and Tactical Flexibility: One area where Slot's innovation stands out is his approach to integrating young players into the system. Slot recognizes that player development goes hand-in-hand with tactical development. He tailors his tactics to suit the strengths of young talents, fostering an environment where they can thrive while executing complex systems. This ability to balance youth development with team success sets him apart from many of his peers.

Practical Lesson for Coaches: Innovation requires a willingness to challenge traditional methods. Be open to experimenting with new tactics and systems, while ensuring your approach aligns with the strengths of your players. In a rapidly changing football landscape, innovation is crucial for sustained success.

4. Commitment to Team Unity: Building Strong Relationships

Slot places a heavy emphasis on building relationships within his squad. His ability to get players to work for each other—both in defence and attack—is a hallmark of his coaching philosophy. By focusing on creating a cohesive unit, Slot maximizes the potential of his squad, encouraging a collective effort rather than relying on individual brilliance.

Communication and Trust: One of Slot's key strengths is his communication. He maintains a clear line of dialogue with his players, ensuring that they understand their roles within the team structure. This transparency fosters trust and unity, which is vital for team chemistry.

The Importance of Teamwork: Whether it's in the high press, where players are required to work in unison to win the ball back, or in offensive transitions, Slot's teams are known for their cohesiveness. He believes that success comes from players working together, supporting each other on and off the pitch.

Practical Lesson for Coaches and Players: Foster a strong sense of unity within your team. Encourage open communication and ensure everyone understands their role and responsibilities. In successful teams, unity is often the difference-maker.

Conclusion

Arne Slot's journey offers a wealth of lessons for anyone involved in football. His leadership, resilience, innovative tactics, and commitment to team unity provide a blueprint for success in modern football. Whether you are a coach, player, or sports enthusiast, Slot's career shows that success is not just about talent but also about the ability to adapt, evolve, and work together towards a common goal.

Printed in Great Britain
by Amazon